POLLEN
AND
FRAGMENTS:

Selected Poetry
and
Prose of Novalis

Translated from the German
with an Introductory Essay
by Arthur Versluis

Phanes Press
1989

To my parents, A. James and Barbara Versluis—and to my great-grandfather Albin and great-grandmother Sophie Preusse, who would have been proud—this book is affectionately dedicated.

© 1989 by Arthur Versluis.

All rights reserved. No part of this publication may be reproduced or transmitted in any form, with the exception of short excerpts used in reviews, without permission in writing from the publisher.

92 91 90 89   4 3 2 1

Published by Phanes Press, PO Box 6114, Grand Rapids, MI 49516, USA.

Library of Congress Cataloging-in-Publication Data

Novalis, 1772-1801.
    [Selections. English. 1989]
    Pollen and fragments : selected poetry and prose of Novalis / translated from the German by Arthur Versluis.
        p. cm.
    Bibliography: p.
    ISBN 0-933999-75-5 (alk. paper) : $25.00. — ISBN 0-933999-76-3 (pbk. : alk. paper) : $12.95
    1. Novalis, 1772-1801—Translations, English.   I. Title.
PT2291.A287   1989   89-34801
831'.6—dc20   CIP

This book is printed on alkaline paper which conforms to the permanent paper standard developed by the National Information Standards Organization.

Printed and bound in the United States

POLLEN AND FRAGMENTS

Contents

Preface 7
Introduction 9

I. APHORISMS AND FRAGMENTS

Pollen 25

Faith and Love or the King and the Queen 41

New Fragments 49
    I. Poeticism 49
    II. Logological Fragments 53
    III. Sophie, or On Woman 57
    IV. Notes on the Margin of Life 63
    V. From the Hidden World 70

The Encyclopedia 81
    I. Philosophy 84
    II. Mathematics and Natural Knowledge 90
    III. Medicine, Psychology 96
    IV. Philology and Art 104
    V. States and Human Patterns 112
    VI. Cosmology and Religion 115

II. SELECTED POETRY

The Stranger 129
Fragment 131
Quo me Bacchus 132
The Boat Journey 133
Cythere 134
The Dying Genius 135
Almighty Spirit, Source of All Being 136
Know Yourself 137
Hymns to the Night 138

Notes and Commentary 161
Bibliography 169

Preface

The work you hold in your hands is one of the most unusual books written in East or West: in their breadth and in their insight, the aphorisms taken as a whole are extraordinarily ambitious and wide ranging. Yet though here and there, in scattered works of the nineteenth and twentieth centuries, one finds reference to the aphorisms, poems and novels of Novalis, no one has yet undertaken the momentous task of collating the various extant versions of the fragments—handwritten and published—and translating them into English. This work is intended, then, as a means of introducing the general reader to Novalis (Friedrich von Hardenberg), both now (when there is no other introduction) and in the future—for even if Novalis' complete works are translated into English, the cost of the volumes shall still make the present work a worthwhile introduction.

This translation is a work born of fascination and of love, and as such has passed through many hands, and many revisions, many expansions, each offering new insights of Novalis, arguably the greatest of the German Romantics. We offer it to the reader in the hope that through it, he too may—despite whatever is not yet pellucid in it—share in the delight of Novalis' vision, that new flowers blossom, and new gems crystalize, born of like minds devoted to unity amid diversity. As Emerson (a mind perhaps closer to Novalis' than any other) once wrote, great minds seem to speak with one voice. That you may hear Novalis', we dedicate this work.

Introduction

> ... few books known to us are more worthy of attention than this.
> —Thomas Carlyle in his *Essay on Novalis*

Friedrich von Hardenberg was born on the second of May, 1772, in Wiederstadt, Germany. His childhood was an insular one: his father, a pious and conservative Moravian, maintained a strict and somber atmosphere in their home, while his mother lavished affection on the children, concealing their faults and egregious thoughts from their father. His father was a rigid man, who wouldn't so much as converse with his neighbors, deeming it unchristian and dangerous. Having read in the newspaper of the French Revolution and its anti-religious sentiment, it is said he threw the paper down in a fury and vowed never to touch one again, a vow which to all reports he kept. It seems likely, in any event, that this veiling of the children's thoughts may have furthered the later rift between them and their father, to whom their—in particular Friedrich's—apparently rebellious and unconventional views came as something of a shock.

And so the children grew up in isolation in the family mansion on the Harz river, in a labyrinthine home which once housed a nunnery—and perhaps it was just this isolation, this childhood in which they were left to their own devices, which began to disclose the manifold inner world to Novalis: the placidity and strictures of his external world were perhaps balanced by a complementary amplification of the inner realm of imagination and myth, glimmers of celestial Reality.

After having argued vehemently with his father over the strict tenets of the Moravians, to which his father staunchly adhered, von Hardenberg left to stay with his uncle, the Landcomthur of Lucklum, whose vast estate and rich library were at his disposal until his departure in 1791 to study law at Jena, one of the most illustrious universities in Germany. In 1793 he left Leipzig to study at Wittenberg, concentrating upon mathematics, chemistry and philosophy. There he met several of the most influential thinkers of his time, became close friends with Schlegel and Fichte, and concluded his academic studies the following year. After having turned down, at his father's insistence, a government position, Novalis assumed a managerial post in the salines, or salt mines near his home, of which his father was director.

At about this time he met Sophie von Kuhn, the thirteen year old girl who became his consuming passion, his Madonna, and he spent a great deal of time at her parents' home, which formed a lively contrast to his own somber and anxious family life. But on March 19, 1797, she died after a protracted illness, and Novalis was griefstricken: her loss drove him even deeper into that inner realm. In late March of that year he wrote to his friend Just, saying: "I shall devote myself to thoughts of the unseen world, and until my death, which cannot be far off, I will seek comfort among a few friends and devotion to my duty." In addition, ever more aware of his own impending death from consumption, he wrote: "Everywhere there is too much noise and bustle for me. I shall retreat into myself more and more. Thus the path to the hereafter will become familiar. The chasm which separates us will become narrower and narrower."

In 1799 Novalis was appointed Assessor of the salines, became close friends with Ludwig Tieck—whom he consulted about all his literary work—and was preparing to marry Julie Charpentier, daughter of the Berghauptmanns von Charpentier. Despite this activity, he was still very frail, and in 1800 he became quite ill. By 1801, having worked feverishly upon his novels and aphorisms, he was scarcely able to write, and on March 25, 1801, at the age of twenty-eight, he died of consumption—tuberculosis. With the exception of a few poems, including *Hymns to the Night*, nearly all of his work was published posthumously under the pseudonym Novalis, by his friends. He had chosen the name Novalis because of its Latin implications—'newly ploughed field'—and because it was a family name on his mother's side.

Though brief, his life encompassed the extremes: it was a life marked by isolation and by close companionship, by consuming passion and by consuming grief, by poetic genius and by success in business, and perhaps most of all by a quest for knowledge—his insatiable need to know spanned all forms of knowledge, from mathematics to poetry, from chemistry to philosophy. Characteristically, paradoxically, his was an eclecticism marked by its depth, its penetration, and he was said by his contemporaries to have been as ingenious in practical matters as in literary: Tieck said that his mind was ever on something new, be it a philosophical or an engineering problem.

Indeed, in his quest for uniting the poles, even the rift between Novalis and his father was ultimately healed—as his post at the salines would indicate—for in a curious roundabout way Novalis' revolutionary journey within led him finally back to the very conservative values with which he began, albeit values infused with a new, theosophic understanding. The essay "Christianity or Europe," and the aphorisms here translated, are not as antithetical as Octavio Paz has suggested, but rather are complementary halves, the essay celebrating the form of Christianity, and the aphorisms celebrating its theophanic content.

Clearly, then, this is the chief characteristic of Novalis' work, for above all, in literature as in life, he sought to conjoin the opposites, to unite the poles, to illuminate that ineluctable Essence, that Light in which the two become one, and which is the true aim of all science, art, philosophy and religion: his writings manifest and reflect that which has been termed the philosopher's stone, the quadrature of the circle, and the ur-ground, and is in fact the Sun of our existence—the absolute union and completeness of the Godhead.

And so we turn to the nature of those works.

* * *

Although, and perhaps because Novalis' works are enigmatic and fragmentary, in reading them one is always aware that they are the expressions of one who knows, of one who is describing an empirical, analogous, unseen but wholly experiential reality. Novalis was certain: even his questions are rhetorical flourishes, inquiries to which he already knew the outlines of the answer. And this is at the heart of Novalis' work: while his mind ranged over every subject available to him—from geognosy to astronomy to dance to psychology to physics to political science to religion to medicine—yet despite his eclecticism, there always lies at the center of his work a Sun, with which he is always in alignment and which in fleeting glimpses is revealed to him—he, in turn, disclosing it to us.

Perhaps the most distinguishing feature of the *Fragments* is their breadth and depth—they range everywhere. There is a reference here, it seems, for virtually anything one can imagine, all drawn together by Novalis' anthropocosmic, Hermetic, rooted vision of life. But underlying Novalis' vision—and suggestive of its ultimate unity—is mathematics, which Plato and Pythagoras also saw as the structure of knowledge. Through mathematical relationships Novalis saw the consonance of this world and another, analogous realm which, by means of logical equations, must be seen to exist, and which is central to Novalis' wide ranging observations.

Hence he spoke in terms of square roots and equations, suggesting for instance that minerals are the Essence to the first power, vegetables the same to the second power, animals are the Essence to the third power, and man is the Essence to the power of Infinity. This vision of existence, which underlies traditional spiritual alchemy, is paralleled in the writings of the Sufi alchemist Jabir ibn Hayyan, who also saw all existence in the traditional way: as gradations of consciousness, its aim being the saint, the holy one. Novalis spoke of plus and minus poetry, of death as the inversion of life—indeed, all human activity seems capable of being expressed in ordered, geometric mathematical patterns, its goal being ordered freedom, orbit around the Sun.

Novalis expressed a coherent unity of thought and action reminiscent of Islamic Sufism: in both one finds references to the King, to the Sun, to the Friends in the Night, to the Guide, to the metaphors of sickness and health, even to the idea of the writing itself as a kind of fragrance or pollen, which one mind sends into the spiritual atmosphere to be wafted here and there until it is received by another mind of kindred spirit. This same idea was poetically expressed by the Islamic poet Farid ud'din

Attar, who dedicated his *Conference of the Birds* to those who through his work encounter that mysterious fragrance of the Divine. The *Diwan* of Hafiz also suggests that its purpose is to act as pollen. This isn't to say that Novalis knew of the Sufis, only that his thought is parallel to theirs. Indeed, Novalis' title, *Pollen and Fragments*, describes well his works: grains of pollen and crystalline 'seeds' dispersed from the flower of one mind in order to propagate manifold forms of beauty and truth, reflections of the Divine. As Novalis put it:

> Flowers are allegories of consciousness or mind. A higher propagation is the aim of the higher flower, a higher preservation: in the human consciousness there is also an organ of immortality, its aim a progressive propagation of the personality. Remarkable inferences and conclusions for both realms.
>
> (*New Fragments*)

In the same way, the fragments are kernels, seeds about which the whole may crystalize. Hence the title denotes the perfection of both content (pollen) and form (crystalline seeds or fragments).

Both his form and content arose from a rooted, traditional, anthropocentric[1] understanding of the cosmos: like Blake, who was in many ways close to him in thought, Novalis was a visionary. But in contrast to Blake, Novalis sought to conjoin everything, to embrace all opposites. Blake was fiercely iconoclastic—as he said in *The Marriage of Heaven and Hell*, his Christ came to cut the world in twain. Novalis' Christ, on the other hand, is the Sun around which all revolves. This is not, of course, to suggest that the two were in any way fundamentally opposed, but rather that they each saw different aspects of the same ineffable truth. And this difference between the two is reflected in their lives: Novalis' Hermetic fragments connote an association of Friends in the Night, of contemporaries including Tieck, Schlegel, Schelling, Fichte, and of course Goethe, who by this time—1798—was immersed in his enigmatic *Diwan*, as well as his fairy-tales and Rosicrucian studies. In short, Novalis, unlike Blake, was in illustrious company and did not have to endure the inward struggle in the same isolated way that Blake did. Undoubtedly, for instance, the brothers Schlegel—one of whom was an Orientalist scholar—contributed much to Novalis' work, as did Goethe and Fichte. But above all, implicit in his work as in his life, is Novalis' aim (not unlike Blake's) of unifying all in magical vision.

This unification also extends to his literary classification, for Novalis includes in his work elements of Platonism, Hermeticism, and Romanticism. Certainly Novalis was the inspiration for many German Romantics after him—the blue flower in his unfinished novel *Heinrich von Ofterdingen* virtually epitomizes Romanticism—but his Romanticism derived from a Platonic basis (though at times he found reason to criticize Plato). Indeed, the following passage could have been written by Novalis:

> It is quite hard to realize that every soul possesses an organ better worth saving than a thousand eyes, because it is our only means of seeing the truth; and that when its light is dimmed or extinguished by other interests, these studies will purify the hearth and rekindle the sacred fire.[2]

Above all, Novalis manifests the Romantic reaction against the modern, mechanistic worldview. Yet like Plato, Novalis affirmed our responsibility to rekindle the sacred fire, and this affirmation is at times difficult to classify.[3]

But certainly Friedrich von Hardenberg stood very much in the Hermetic, Pythagorean, alchemical current, according to which this world reflects the Divine, unseen realm, and is governed and informed by mathematical principles and proportions. According to this tradition, often associated also with the term Christian Kabbalah, man's purpose is not to attain technological domination of the earth, but to realize his origin and purpose, and to live in harmony with nature. In this tradition, perhaps best identified by association with names like Eckhart, Tauler, Ruysbroeck, Boehme, St. Martin and von Baader, our purpose is—in Novalis' words—"to become as our Father is."[4]

Man, a microcosm, is bound to become God, to conjoin nature and spirit, to take true possession of his organs and senses, thereby realizing the Spirit upon earth. Throughout Novalis' work one finds alchemical, Hermetic echoes. The poem "Know Yourself" is wholly alchemical in imagery and theme—alchemy being a physical expression of spiritual transmutation. For Novalis,

> Paradise is strewn over the earth—and therein has become unknown. Its scattered lineaments are bound to coalesce—its skeleton is bound to become enfleshed. Regeneration of paradise.
> (*The Encyclopedia*)

This thought is closely paralleled in the early Christian *Gospel of Thomas*, as well as in the teachings of certain Kabbalistic and Hermetic Christian sects, as well for that matter as in Mahayana Buddhist teachings: it suggests that our responsibilities toward the soul, toward nature, and toward the inner realm are far greater than we now acknowledge. To what extent, asks Novalis, is the duty of man to be compassionate with God—as God—lost to Western man? Yet there are few traces of *apocalyptic* Christianity here: rather, Novalis focuses on the inward path in an almost Taoist way, as in this description of the best citizens:

> Quick to mention all good qualities, they laugh silently over the tomfoolery of their contemporaries and contain themselves concerning their evil. They don't seek to rectify error because they know that each correction of this kind, and under such premisses, is only a new error, and the best cannot come from outside. They abandon all rank and title, and so are not troubled—and so they trouble no one, and are everywhere welcome.
> (*Faith and Love*)

In truth, it often appears that Novalis, with the full scope of Occidental Hermeticism behind him, reached conclusions remarkably parallel to more fully developed Oriental teachings —almost as if he was directing his work toward a union of Orient and Occident. Undeniably many if not all of the essential teachings of Mahayana Buddhism are to be found in the *Fragments*. Among the aphorisms are references to the compassionate one (in Buddhism termed the *bodhisattva*), to the ineradicability of *karma*, or fate, to the ultimately inseparable union of the transcendent and the immanent (in Buddhist terms *nirvana* and *samsara*), and above all to the fundamental truth of egolessness. As Novalis said,

> The true philosophical act is the slaying of the self; this is the real beginning of all philosophy, therein lies the requirement for all philosophic youths, and only this act answers all criteria and conditions for the transcendental deed.
> *(Logological Fragments)*

In religion and philosophy, as in literature, Novalis transcends mere labels and superficial distinction—just as he combines elements from various Hermetic, Pythagorean, Platonic and other currents of thought, so in his work one sees parallels with Oriental teachings. For the parallels with Mahayana Buddhism and with Vedanta in his thoughts are due neither to chance nor to significant contact with Orientalists, but rather to the fact that the reality which Novalis glimpsed can *ultimately* be no different from that realized in Buddhist and Hindu traditions. The difference is one of degree, not kind, and is due in part to cultural coloring. René Gérard, in his study of the Orient in German Romanticism, makes note of precisely this parallelism between Novalis' observations and Vedanta.[5] But of course Novalis remains within, finally, the Western Platonic tradition.

At the heart of the *Fragments* is the view that man's potential is infinite: although he is at present sick, or asleep, or trapped in the cave of matter, it is possible and in fact essential for him to awaken, to amplify his temporal senses and to realize his eternal true nature—for, paradoxically, awareness of the sensual and of the eternal are indivisibly linked. We are in the process of becoming human, of becoming Divine. Often Novalis seems to be alluding to a means toward this end, to a system—as in the passages on health and illness, or in the references to meditative awareness—yet these observations are wary and elusive as deer: one only captures fleeting glimpses.

While affirming that the body is a limitation, a boundary, Novalis yet celebrated it, affirming that "when we touch another human being, we touch heaven," and insisting that the development of absolute sensation was concurrent with the unfolding of the soul, observing that to wake up here is to wake up in the higher realm. The fruit of paradox, of transcending duality, these aphorisms and poems present one with ever new angles of vision.

Though Novalis drew upon and stood within the Christian tradition and symbology, his vision of it, like that of Blake and that of Emerson, was from a transformative point of view: our task, he said in several passages—frightening in their implications for our true responsibilities—is to become like our Father, to manifest the Divine, to incarnate Heaven. The modern mind, enmeshed far more in the dark Satanic mills than even Blake anticipated, draws back in the face of such demands.

There is a sense, though, in which all great thinkers have made the same demands, have thought with one mind and spoken with but one voice: that sense is heightened in *Fragments*, for the aphorisms seem like shimmering bits of crystal which formed naturally, spontaneously—as if they were precipitates from an ethereal realm, for which Novalis was only a catalyst. In a very real sense all the *Fragments* are variations upon a theme: as Novalis says, there is but one truth, with myriad contrasting expressions of it.

In *The Encylopedia* Novalis wrote that one should, when overwhelmed by the shadow of a giant, move aside and see if the colossal shadow isn't merely that of a pygmy blocking out the Sun. In an age dominated by pygmies blocking out the Sun, it comes as little surprise that Novalis' shadow is relatively small: while regarded as influential, little of his work has been translated. But he cast no shadow only because he sought to reveal the Sun rather than to block it out.

And yet he made his presence felt: one senses his influence in Rilke, in Hesse, and more subtly in many others. But without a doubt, like a passing comet his ultimate influence—and the influence of that which inspired him—upon the planets which we call humanity has not yet been fully registered: perhaps, still, there are earthquakes, climatic changes, and rebirths yet to occur.

Because the central theme of Novalis' work is unity, he insists upon acceptance and amplification of the world and of both poles. Saint and sinner are one. This is perhaps best signified by his use of the word *Wollust*, which he saw as characterizing religion in general, and true Christianity in particular. *Wollust* is a word implying lascivious sexual pleasure, as well as bliss and ecstatic delight: it clearly unites in one word Christianity's greatest grace—ecstasy—and perhaps its greatest aversion—the apple of sexual knowledge. Sin, Novalis asserts, is but the urge toward the Godhead. Through such paradoxes Novalis points toward a consciousness beyond the merely individual, and all his poetry and prose are in at least one sense descriptions of a residue from this exalted state, which Plato, after all, found as the chief characteristic of poets of his day.

However, the word *Wollust* also brings to mind a question, one which is directly related to the following aphorism:

> It is peculiar that the association of ecstasy, religion, and the ferocity of the people has not long since been made, considering their inner kinship and the familiarity of the tendencies.
> *(The Encyclopedia)*

What is the relationship between ecstasy or *Wollust*, and the ferocity of the crowd? Is the implication that individual ecstasy contributes to the ferocity of the crowd? If so, then Novalis might be seen as advocating—since he clearly is an ecstatic poet and philosopher—a variant form of fascism. After all, he often speaks of the unity of man and state, of microcosm and macrocosm: a superficial case might be made positing such an argument. But the juxtaposition would be quite mistaken. For in fact, Novalis was warning of the possible dangers to those who aspire to ecstasy—he was warning them of the fate of Giordano Bruno and Christ and al-Hallaj, the Sufi who said "I am the truth" in a moment of bliss, and was subsequently drawn and quartered by an enraged Islamic mob.

All of these martyrs, like Novalis himself, emphasized the necessity of slaying the self, of realizing the inherent emptiness of ego. Those in the mob, on the other hand, bolster their ego through identification with the masses, naturally focussing their rage upon anyone who stands out and, not incidentally, upon those who stand for the slaying of the self. In short, Novalis was in the aphorism quoted above, warning of the dangers of one polarity—the highest mysticism—often exciting in others the opposite polarity—the ferocity of the masses. In Neoplatonic or Hermetic terms the masses or matter attempt to drag down the spirit, pulling it here and there. Far from advocating a variant form of fascism, Novalis was in fact anticipating its recurrence in the future, for it is the natural result of the ego's triumph, the essential irreality of which men like Novalis must constantly reiterate.[6]

And so Novalis' political discussions, like his geognosy and his astronomy, were not only literal, but figurative and allusive as well, a means of illustrating spiritual reality. If his unified political state is—like any of his work—taken only in its literal meaning then, as Novalis wryly notes in another context, the reader is "a wholly honorable man only if he doesn't pass himself off as a poet." Says Novalis:

> The King is the pure life-principle of the state; he is, therefore, precisely what the sun is to the planets.
> *(Faith and Love or the King and the Queen)*

The King, then, spiritually animates his citizens, illuminating them like the sun, an observation which can be taken both in an inner and in an outer way. Essentially, we find in Novalis' politics a kind of theocracy, in which the King and Queen have spiritual power or import, and a distrust of revolution, which often proves itself but destructive energy, creating new infirmity in a nation. And both of these ideas—theocracy, and distrust of revolution—may be interpreted spiritually as well as literally.

In truth, no matter what Novalis is discussing, be it chemistry, physics or poetry, his discussion often has several levels of meaning, meanings often so ethereal that they excite a flash of insight only to be lost with the onset of discursive thought. Like much Oriental art—particularly Zen Buddhist and Taoist—Novalis' *Fragments*, his poetry and his novels, like his life, only appear to be unfinished. Novalis, much like a Taoist painter, often chose this fragmentary form deliberately—even to planning an unfinished poem to end his unfinished novel—in order to allow the reader to fill in the gaps, to leap the synapses within the work. For in reading the *Fragments*, one encounters spaces across which the mind leaps, thereby attaining a flash of recognition unavailable to one reading continuous, unbroken prose, prose having a more completed, rounded quality. In this way the work, and the higher reality of which it is a reflection and an expression, is assimilated by the reader in a way not ordinarily accessible to us. Read properly, Novalis' works—like a Taoist painting, or a Zen Buddhist poem—elicit a brief glimpse of Reality. As he put it:

> In each touch arises a substance which works as long as the touch continues. This is the ground for all synthetic modifications of the individual. There is either one-sided, or reciprocal touching. The hereafter confirms this.
>
> (*Pollen*)

There is a void within many of these aphorisms, and many times the reader must complete the thought, making it whole as an allusive and delicate *sumi* painting is made whole. This emptiness within the art work—so that the work must be completed by each reader or viewer individually—is at the heart of all Oriental art, and is based upon the recognition that each person must come to realize the truth for himself. If Novalis' works sometimes appear inaccessible, it is often because one has not arced across that inner synapse, and gained that inner recognition of the Reality he is conveying.

Of course, Novalis' aphorisms were often jotted down as notes for a much greater work which he could not complete (his grand plans for a universal encyclopedia cut short by his untimely death), and weren't all intended for publication. The aphorisms were gathered together by Novalis' literary executor, Tieck, and so are in various stages of completion.[7] Hence at times the punctuation indicates haste, and we left this so in the translation; at other times the poet simply jotted notes he might elaborate further, notes which to us may be perplexing. This sketchiness creates certain difficulties for the reader, but at the same time it seems appropriate for this poet who completed so little in his life, and who began so much. What is more, it adds a certain excitement to the reading, for we, in 'filling the gaps,' must learn also, and contribute.

In any case, though Novalis' prose is cryptic, and though he often seems almost out of our view, above the mists and in the sunny heights of the mountains, yet the glimpses he affords of those heights are of great value. Many of his insights seem uncannily current: one thinks of his insistence upon the earth as being ONE good, or upon the eventual primacy of chemical astronomy or physics,[8] or upon the myth and the fairy-tale as the repository of all archetypal knowledge—all these are current because they are always current. Like Thoreau, Novalis read not the times, but the eternities. His Pierian Spring was that most ancient of wells: the Mystery which the Egyptian, Chaldean, Orphic, Dionysian and Eleusinian celebrants sought—and which certainly at least some of them found.

Novalis stood on the verge of the modern era, but he was still influenced by and in many ways epitomized the Renaissance model of the whole man, who had the key to all knowledge and sciences, one who was successful publicly and privately, in literature and science and business. Like another transcendentalist—Emerson—Novalis sought to play all the parts: he sought to conquer with vigor every sphere of life. In so doing, he sowed many seeds. And as he noted at the beginning of *Pollen and Fragments*:

> Friend, the ground is poor; we must strew abundant seed, that we might nonetheless reap a modest harvest.

Perhaps more of the seeds Novalis strewed took root than he imagined.

Periodically, the *sophia perennis* for which Novalis is an eloquent, a brilliant spokesman, resurges—and perchance its time has come again.

—Arthur Versluis

I. Aphorisms and Fragments

Pollen

Friends, the ground is poor; we must strew abundant seed that we might nonetheless reap a modest harvest.

We seek above all the Absolute, and always find only things.[1]
1

The designation through tone and line is a wonderful abstraction. Three letters designate the word 'God;' a single line reveals a million things. How free becomes the operation of the universe here; how vivid the concentricity of the spirit-world! One command mobilizes the armies; a word affects the freedom of nations.
2

The world-state is the body which the beautiful world, the companion world, inspires. The body is its indispensable organ.
3

Apprenticeship for poetical youths; academic years for philosophical youths. Academe should be a thoroughly philosophical institution: only one faculty, the whole arrangement organized to stimulate and to practically exercise the mind's power.
4

Apprenticeships in the superior sense are apprenticeships to living art. Through systematic, ordered endeavors, one learns to know underlying principles, and to retain this accomplishment, after which one chooses how to proceed.
5

We never come to comprehend ourselves wholly, but we

will and can do far more than comprehend.

6

The distinction between illusion and reality lies in the difference between their life-functions. Illusion lives upon reality; reality lives its life in itself. One annihilates illusion as one annihilates sickness, and hence conquering illusion is nothing but logical ignition or extinction, ecstasy or philistinism. Illusion usually leaves behind an apparent deficiency in the mind's power, which nothing short of a decreasing dosage of an induced remedy will alleviate.[2] These (who have been cured of the original illusion) often exhibit a deceptive liveliness, whose dangerous revolutionary symptoms can only become dispelled through successive vigorous remedies. Both dispositions can come to change only through constant, strict adherence to treatment.

7

The highest is the most comprehensible, the nearest, the most indispensable.

8

Life is the beginning of death. Life is for death's sake. Death is the end, and a beginning as well, a separation and yet closer to a reunion with Self. Through death the Reduction is consummated.

9

Imagination places the future world either in the realms above us or in the realms below us,[3] or in our metempsychosis toward ourselves. We dream of journeys through the cosmos: isn't the cosmos then in ourselves? The depths of our spirits we know not. —Toward the Interior goes the arcane way. In us, or nowhere, is the Eternal with its worlds, the past and future. The outer world is a shadow world, which casts its shadow into the realm of light. Now it appears, to be sure, inside us as darkness, solitary and formless, but how utterly different will it appear when this darkening is past and the shadow-body is transcended.

We enjoy it more each time because our spirit has been deprived.

10

Darwin[4] observed that we are less blinded by the light upon awakening if we have dreamt the visible objects. I dare say that we dream here, in fact, from seeing beyond! Blessed are those who have already dreamt of seeing. They will sooner be able to bear the Glory of the world beyond.

11

To what extent can a human being have a sense for something, if he doesn't have its embryo inside him? Whatever I come to understand must itself develop organically in myself, and what I seem to learn is only nourishment and cultivation of that inner organism.

12

The seat of the soul is there, where the inner world and the outer world touch. Where they permeate each other, the seat is in every point of the permeation.

13

Genius is the capacity to treat imaginary objects as real, and to even manipulate them as such. The talent of describing, of observing exactly—appropriate for describing one's observations—is distinct from genius. Without this talent, however, one sees only half, and is only half genius; one can have a capacity for genius which never comes to be developed due to a deficiency of these talents.

14

Shame is indeed a feeling of profanation. Intimacy, love and piety should be handled privately; one should speak of them only in rare moments of trust, a tacit understanding then arising. Many things are too delicate to be thought, much less spoken of in words.

15

Self-renunciation is the source of all abasement, just as it is the ground of all true exaltation. The first step is to gaze into the Interior—secluding contemplation of oneself. Whoever remains here has attained only half. The second step must be to actively gaze outward, in steady, spontaneous observation of the outer world.

16

The highest duty of education is to take possession of one's transcendental self, to master the ego. For so few, strangely, is there a need for a complete sense of and understanding for another. Apart from complete self-knowledge, one will never truly learn to understand another.

17

The insignificant, mundane, raw, loathsome and ill-bred becomes through witticism alone fit for companionship. It is as if these were intended only as jokes: their destined aim is to be a joke.

18

We are on a mission: toward cultivating the earth are we summoned.

19

If a spirit appeared to us, then we ourselves would take possession of that singular spiritual state: we are inspired inasmuch as we and the spirit are together. Apart from inspiration, there is no appearance of spirit. Inspiration is appearance and reflection, appropriation and communication together.

20

Man lives and works only in the Ideal, through the enhancement of its presence. For the time being, there is no other means for spiritual working in this world. Accordingly, it is one's duty to think of the dead. It is the only way to remain with them in the mundane world. God himself is in no other way available to

us than through faith.
21

Who might have invented wit? Every quality of our mind which has been brought to our consciousness is in the truest sense a newly discovered world.
22

The spirit always appears in strange, evanescent forms.
23

Now the spirit stirs only here and there: when will the spirit stir the whole? When will humanity begin to remember itself?
24

Man abides in truth. As one prizes truth, so one cherishes oneself. Whoever betrays truth, betrays himself. We speak not of lies here, but rather of acts against convictions.
25

In serene souls there is no jesting. Jesting indicates a loss of equilibrium; it is both a succession of disturbances, and the center's restoration. The sharpest wit has passion. The condition of the dissolution of all proportion—despair and spiritual death—is most fearfully witty.
26

We cling to lifeless matter because of its connections, its solid form. We love matter insofar as it is connected with the beloved Essence, insofar as these traces reach, or insofar as the material object resembles or reflects the Beloved.
27

The object of maintaining a fellowship is nothing but to be a means of resuscitation, revival. This determines its selection, its variations, and its means of treatment. The association is nothing but a mutual life: an indivisible thinking and feeling person. Each person is an association in miniature.

28

To retreat within ourselves means to withdraw from the outer world. Among the spirits this earthly life, analogically, is an inner observation, a withdrawing into oneself, an immanent effecting. So this earthly life arises from an incipient reflection, a primeval withdrawing or containment, germinating in oneself, that is as free as our reflection. Conversely, the spiritual life arises in this world from a breakthrough of each original reflection.[5] The spirit unfolds itself afresh, emanating itself anew here, preserving the former reflection, and in this moment it says 'I' for the first time. One sees here how relative the terms 'going out' and 'coming in,' or expansion and contraction, are. What we term 'coming in' is actually 'going out,' a recurrent resumption of the original Form.

29

Error and bias are burdens, indirectly attracting remedies, as every load balances. For the frail they are certainly a weakening agent.

30

A people is an idea. We should become a people. A consummate, completed person is a people in miniature. True popularity is the highest aim of man.

31

Each step of development begins with childhood. Therefore earthly man is taught the most, for he so resembles a child.

32

Every beloved object is the focus of a paradise.

33

The individual only *interests* one; hence everything classical

is not individual.
34

The true letter (*der Brief*) is, after its own nature, poetic.
35

The impulse toward association is the impulse toward organization. Through this spiritual assimilation arises often here, from common components, an excellent association about a completed man.
36

The most interesting is the material which excites beauty about it. Where spirit and beauty are, the best of all nature amasses in concentrated oscillations.
37

The best of knowledge is its philosophical ingredients, which are as life is to an organic body. One dephilosophizes knowledge: what more remains? Earth, air and water.
38

Humanity is a humorous role.
39

Law courts, theater, palace, farm, church, government, official assemblies, academies and colleges and so forth are all, as it were, special inner organs of the mystic state-individual.
40

All which befalls our lives is material, from which we can make what we will. Whoever has more spirit, makes more from his life. Each acquaintance, each occurrence, becomes from the spiritual vista the first movement of an unending progression, beginning an unending novel.
41

A translation is either grammatical or changing or mythical. Mythic translations are translations in the highest style. They represent clearly the complete character of the individual artworks. They don't give us the actual work, but rather its Ideal. Yet there exists, I trust, no whole model thereof. Many critiques and descriptions of artworks affect one in spirit with but brilliant traces of the original. Mythic translation requires a mind in which the poetic spirit and the philosophic spirit have been mastered in their full abundance. Greek mythology is to some extent such a translation of a national religion. What's more, the modern Madonna is such a myth.

Grammatical translations are translations in the customary sense. They afford much erudition, but engage only discursive faculties.

Variable translations, because they should be genuine, require the highest poetic spirit. They easily fall into travesty, as did Bürger's Homer in iambic verse, Pope's Homer, and the French translations collectively. The true translation of this kind must be in the artist's own day, and the idea of the whole settled upon, given to be understood. In an analogous way stands the Genius of humanity to each individual person.

Not merely books, but all can undergo these three kinds of translation.

42

In the highest sorrow there occurs at times a paralysis of the sensibility. The soul disintegrates. Hence the deathly frost courts the mind's power, and the perpetual wit of such a one resounds with despair. No inclination is left; man then stands alone as a destructive power. Disconnected with the rest of the world, he gradually consumes himself, becoming in principle, misanthropic and misotheistic.

43

Our language is either mechanistic, atomistic or dynamic. Genuine poetic speech, however, should be living, organic. How often we perceive the poverty of words when trying to strike a

wealth of ideas with a single blow.
44

Poet and priest were in the beginning one, and only later ages have separated them. The highest poet is always a priest, just as the highest priest is always but a poet of faith. And shouldn't the future life induce anew the ancient state?
45

Writings are the thoughts of states; archives are their memories.
46

The more we purify our senses, the more suited they become to individual characteristics. The highest sense could be the highest receptivity for individual nature. The establishment of individual talent would correspond to the individual's relative skill and energy. Inasmuch as one's intent is manifested in this sense—individually—so generate the passions for or against individuality: love and hate. Mastery in play characterizes one who discerns these senses in himself through the ruling understanding.
47

The basis of all eternal bonding is an absolute tendency toward universal alignment. Thereupon rests the power of the hierarchy, the true Masonry, and the hidden bond of all genuine thinkers. Herein lies the possibility of a universal republic, which the Romans, up to the Caesars, had begun to realize. First Augustus lost this basis, and Hadrian destroyed it wholly.
48

In the primeval time of the discovery of the capacity for discernment, each new judgement was a find. The value of these finds increased, the more applicable and fruitful they were. To judge and to sentence, which to us has become quite commonplace, was in those days still an unfamiliar stage in the life of understanding. One had to summon genius and sagacity in order to meet new circumstances by means of new implements. Applying this to the most characteristic, to the most interesting, and to the most common aspects of human life must have above all excited the admiration and drawn the attention of all good minds, of the cultured. Thus too appear gnomic sayings, those which in all times and amongst all peoples are esteemed so highly. It may well be possible that a similar destiny would meet our present ingenious discoveries in the course of the times. There may well come a time when today's thoughts become commonplaces, and the restless spirit of humanity is occupied with newly exalted discoveries.

49

A law is effective according to its conception. An ineffective law is no law. Law is a causal conception, a mingling of power and thought. Hence one is never aware of laws as such.

Insofar as one thinks about a law, it is only a theorem; that is, a thought allied with possibility. An opposing, a tenacious thought is an aspiring one, and reconciles the law with mere thought.

50

The flight of the spirit of consensus is death.

51

In most religious systems we are regarded as members of the Godhead. Hence if one doesn't obey the impulses of the whole, if one doesn't even intentionally act against the law of the whole, but rather only follows one's own course, and will not be a member, then from the Godhead emanates a healing power, and either the wound is healed, or it will be utterly excised.

52

An intimate community of all knowledge, a scientific republic, is the lofty aim of the learned.

53

Shouldn't the distance of a particular science from the common knowledge, and hence the rank of the sciences amongst themselves, be taken into account according to the number of their axioms?

The fewer the axioms, the higher the science.

54

One usually understands the artistic better than the natural. There is more spirit in the simple than in the complicated, but less talent.

55

Implements equip humanity. One can truly say that man understands how to produce a world; he lacks only a suitable apparatus, only the proper use of his sensory instruments. The beginning is there. In the same way, the principles of warships lie in the ideas of the shipmasters, and they are incorporated through crowds and suitable implements and materials into a monstrous machine. So the idea often requires an instant of colossal organization, huge masses of material, and the man is—where not actually, for all that potentially, creator.

56

In each touch arises a substance which works so long as the touch continues. This is the ground for all synthetic modification of the individual. There is either one-sided or reciprocal touching. The former confirms the latter.

57

The more ignorant one is by nature, the more one's capacity for knowledge. Each new perception makes a more profound and living impression. One observes this clearly by an entry into a new field of knowledge. But after a point, one loses through too much studying. Then the primal ignorance is simply being opposed to another kind of ignorance. One is an ignorance from a deficiency of knowledge, the other is the ignorance of an overflow of knowledge. The latter usually fosters the symptoms of skepticism. It is but an unreal skepticism, a more indirect weakness of our capacity to know. One is incapable of penetrating the substance of a matter, and of experiencing it in a specific form: the formative power doesn't suffice. For this reason the visionary spirit of discovery in the younger minds, as well as the auspicious knowledge of the inspired beginner or layman, is easily understandable.

58

Worlds are not built enough on the profound and urgent sense:
But a living heart satisfies the striving spirit.

59

We stand in relationship with all components of the universe, as well as with the hereafter and with antiquity. Which relationships we will cultivate, which for us is preëminently important, and which should be realized, depends only upon the course and duration of our watchfulness.[6] A true method for such proceedings could be no less than that long-awaited art of discovery: it might be even more than this. Man seeks constantly after higher laws, and the possibility of finding them through the genius of introspection is indisputable.

60

Historians organize historical reality. Historical data are the material, which the historian gives form through re-animation. Hence even history stands under the principles of re-animation and organization, and if these aren't there, then there isn't even true historical form, but rather nothing more than—here and there—traces of accidental animation where, involuntarily, genius took power.

61

Before abstraction all is one, but one as chaos; after abstraction, all is again united, but this union is free and independent, a self-determined reality. Out of a multitude a fellowship is born;

in a meaningful world chaos is transfigured.

62

If this world is, as it were, a precipitation of human nature, so is the God-world a sublimation thereof. Both occur as one in actuality. There is no precipitation apart from sublimation. What yonder by dint of its agility wanders forlorn, here will be won.

63

Certainty of themselves and of the unseen powers were the basis of spiritual societies to the present day.

64

A criminal cannot complain about wrongs done him because one treats him harshly and inhumanely. His offense was an entry into the realm of violence, power and tyranny. There is no restraint and proportion in that realm, and therefore he should not be surprised at the disproportion of its counter-reaction.

65

Mythology holds the history of the archetypal world, which contains past, present and future.

66

There are many anti-revolutionary books written in favor of the Revolution. But Burke has written a revolutionary book against the Revolution.[7]

67

What a worthy wish, is it not, to be a modern, a truly great man! The majority of Germans are not of this opinion, however. It is excellent enough to deny all great ways and to follow the baser system. Hence the Copernican system wasn't accepted until it became convenient to relate the sun and the stars anew to the earth, and the earth to the universe. For this reason Goethe, who now is the true representative of the poetic spirit of earth, will be commonly treated and scornfully regarded, because he doesn't deliver the masses' anticipated commonplace amusements, and he reflects their instant of confusion and embarrassment back upon them. An interesting symptom of this weakness of the soul is the reception which 'Hermann and Dorothea' received.

68

The geognostics believe that the physical center of gravity lies under Fez, Morocco. Goethe, as anthropognost, is of the opinion, in 'Wilhelm Meister,' that the intellectual center of gravity lies under the German nation.

69

The human world is the commonplace organ of God. Poetry conjoins us to God, as it conjoins us to one another.

70

Calm plainly appears, in regard to the outer world, as that which is immovable, unchanging. As manifold as its changes may be, as long as it still endures in reference to the outer world it is always calm. This law applies to all self-modification. Therefore beauty appears peaceful. All beauty is a self-illuminated, consummated individual.

71

The more narrow-minded a system is, the more it is pleasing to the world-wise. The system of the materialists, the models of Helvetius, and even Locke have received applause from these classes. Hence Kant always will have more hangers-on than Fichte.

72

The human world is the common organ of the Gods. Poesy unites them, as us.

73

To write books as art—that is not yet discovered. Such

books are yet to be invented. Fragments of this kind are but literary seeds. There may be many barren grains amongst them: nonetheless, imagine—if only a single one sprouts!
74

Addenda

In the *Atheneum* and other places: handwritten and published fragments.

The spirit leads to proof of an eternal self.
75

Death is a self-conquering—that is, as all vanquish the self, all attain a newer, freer existence.
76

We are waking up when we dream that we are dreaming.
77

When man can come no farther, then he is helped by a command, or by a mighty act—a swift resolution.
78

Full of spirit is that wherein the spirit is unceasingly revealed—at all events it often appears afresh, in an unchanging Form again.[8] Not merely a onetime occurrence—something in the beginning—as in most philosophical systems.
79

The transcendental viewpoint for this life awaits us—only from it does life become genuinely meaningful.
80

The most ingenious insight is discerning the proper employment of insight.
81

Whoever will consider fragments of this kind literally may be a thoroughly honorable man—only he should not pass himself off as a poet. Must one then always be mindful? Whoever is too old to revel avoids the more youthful assemblies. Now are the literary saturnalias. The more colorful life is, the better.
82

Schlegel's writings are lyric philosophy. His 'Forster' and 'Lessing' are excellent minus-poetry, and resemble Pindar's Odes. The lyric writer must come to write logical epigrams. He is so wholly drunk with life that it comes to be dithyrambic, which of course one must nourish and evaluate through dithyrambs. An artwork must be half enchanted—in wholly enchanted ones the artwork dissolves—from the human comes an animal—and the animal's character is dithyrambic. The animal's is an oversatisfied life—the plant's is a deficient life—the human's is a free life.
83

Goethe's philosophy is truly epic.
84

Each individual is the midpoint of an emanation-system.
85

If the Spirit hallows it, every true book is a Bible.
86

Where children are, there is a golden age.
87

Faith and Love
or
the King and the Queen

Prologue

If one intends to speak of something secret with a few others, when one is in a greater, diffused society, and the group is not close together, then one must discourse in an extraordinary language. This extraordinary language can be either in overtones, or after the image of a foreign language. The latter proves to be a metaphorical or cryptic language.
88

The mystical expression is more an attracting thought. All truth is primeval. The charm of its newness lies only in the variation of expression. The more contrasting its manifestations, the greater the strangeness of the renewed knowledge.[9]
89

Whatever one loves, one finds everywhere, and everywhere sees resemblances and analogies to it. The greater one's love, the vaster and more meaningful is this analogous world. My beloved is the abbreviation of the universe, the universe an elongation, an extrapolation of my beloved. The knowledgeable friend offers all flowers and gifts to his beloved.
90

But from whence arises the earnest, the mystic-political philosophy? An inspired one's utterances reflect the higher life in all his functions: thus he also philosophizes poetically, in a manner yet more enlivened than usual. Even the tones of the symphony are due to its power and organization.[10] But isn't the universe won through the individual, in proportion as the

individual is realized through the universal?
> 91

> Let the dragon-flies rise; innocent strangers they are,
> Follow the twin-star, exulting, with gifts, this way.[11]
> 92

> A blossoming land is surely wholly a kingly artwork, like a park. An elegant park is an English invention. A land with its heart and spirit liberated may become a German invention, and the inventor will surely be king of all creation.
> 93

> If tomorrow I became a prince, I'd entreat the King first for an eudiometer like his own. No instrument is more necessary for princes. I, like he, would seek to draw the vital air for my state more from blossoming plantings than from extracting saltpeter.
> 94

> Gold and silver are the blood of the states. An abundance of blood in either heart or head reveals frailty in both. The more vigorous the heart is, the more liberal and enlivened surges the blood back to the outer extremities. Each limb is warmed and invigorated, and swift and mighty the blood charges back toward the heart.
> 95

> A collapsing throne is like a falling mountain which shatters the plain. A dead sea is left behind where there once was a fruitful land and a delightful, healthy state.
> 96

> Its power equivalent only to that of the mountain, you should be grateful to the ocean. The ocean is the element of freedom and equality. Nevertheless, one is warned to tread upon the layer of fool's gold (iron pyrite); otherwise the volcano

(Vulcan) is there, and with it (him) the origin of new continents.[12]

97

The mephitic, stinking vapor of the moralistic world restrains and hinders like its namesake in nature. Each advances gladly in the heights, while the mists hover near the base. For the dwellers in the heights, there is no better remedy for vapors than the flowers and sunshine. Both are rarely found together in the heights. Upon each of the moral ascensions one can—even now—enjoy the purest breezes, and see a lily in the sun.

98

It was no wonder when the mountains for the most part thundered downward into the valleys and devastated the plains. Ill clouds often lingered about the mountains there, and hid from them their origin above; then the flatlands appeared only as a darker abyss, over which the clouds seemed to endure. The clouds then appearing as an enraged, rising ocean—which, however, was not rising against the mountains in particular—and which gradually dulled and blunted the mountains by erosion, though they were only being swept under by apparently faithful clouds.[13]

99

The King is the pure life-principle of the state; he is, therefore, precisely what the sun is to the planets. Above all, there generates about the life-principle here within the highest life of the state, an atmosphere of light. It is more or less likewise in each citizen. The appearance of the citizens in the King's proximity becomes lustrous, and as poetic as possible, so that they utter expressions of the highest animation and there the highest spiritual animation takes place. The spirit's effects are reflections, but the consummate or beautiful reflection is an image of the essence, and is always conjoined with the highest animation. So the citizens' expressions in the King's presence become those of the highest, steadily returned exuberance, of the liveliest emotion, governed through attentive presence of mind, and the proper regulation of conduct. Without etiquette, no court can last. There is but one natural etiquette—the most beautiful—and one feigning the stylish is hideous. Restoration of the first will be no trivial concern for thoughtful Kings, for through etiquette the citizens both become significantly more refined, and manifest their love for the monarchic form.

100

It is a gross failing of our state that one can see so little of it. Above all, the state should be visible, each man characterized as a citizen. Shouldn't one order the introduction of insignia and uniforms throughout? Whoever considers something so trifling, knows not the essential individuality of our nature.

101

The ancient hypothesis that comets were flames from revolutions in planetary systems holds true, certainly, for another kind of comet, which periodically revolutionizes and rejuvenates the spiritual world-system. The spiritual astronomer notes for some time the influx of such a comet into an important component of the spiritual planets, which we term humanity. Mighty floods, changes in climate, variations in the center of gravity, general tendencies to flee; singular meteors are the symptoms of these violent incidents, the effect of which is that a new world-age is created. As it is necessary, perhaps, that in certain periods all is brought forth in flux, inevitably mixed, and a newer, purer crystallization arises, so is it essential that something moderate this crisis and hinder the planet's total dissolution. Therefore a core remains, a kernel, in order that the new mass may crystalize, and about it new, beautiful forms arise. The solids draw firmly together, the overflowing heated masses diminish, and one spares no remedy to forestall the softening of the bones, the unraveling of the fibers and tissues.

Would it not be madness to make a permanent crisis, and to

trust the feverish condition over the truly healthy state, the preservation of which all must favor? Whoever desires to prolong such a state in crisis—doubt his beneficence, and his efficacy.

102

Won't the King prove to be so through the intimate touch of His Worth?

103

The King and the Queen protect the monarchy better than 200,000 men.

104

Nothing is more invigorating than our wish to speak, because it is already impregnated, already fulfilled.

105

In our time the true wonder of transubstantiation has come to pass. Isn't the court transmuted into a family, a throne into a holy place, and a kingly marriage into an eternal bonding of the heart?

106

When the dove becomes eagle's beloved companion, then the golden age is near, or already there, even when it is not openly recognized and disseminated.

107

Whoever now wishes to see eternal tranquility, and wishes to win love, journeys to Berlin and sees the Queen. There can each be convinced of the obvious: that one must love the eternal, heartfelt tranquility of righteousness above all else, and only through this are we loosed from the perpetual shackles.

108

Addenda

The ground of all folly in conviction and opinion is confusing the ends with the means.
109

Most revolutionaries neither exactly know—nor knew—what they want: Form or Unform.
110

Revolutions soon prove to be against the true energy of a nation. There is an energy of sickness and infirmity—which works more violently than the true—but which itself injures, leaving one with still deeper infirmities.
111

When one passes judgement upon a nation, one evaluates for the most part only the principle evidence, the striking elements of that nation.
112

The more infirm a component is, the more inclined it is to disorder and inflammation.

What are slaves? Utterly weak, compressed people. What are sultans? Through vigorous attractions, they gather slaves. How do sultans and slaves end? Violently. The former nimble as sultans, the latter nimble as slaves—both are frenetic, rabid. How can slaves be cured? Through very cautiously being set free and enlightened. One must handle them as if they were frostbitten. Sultans? In this wise: as Dionysius and Kroesus were cured. With fear, fasting and the restraint of the cloister one begins, and one ascends gradually, using restoratives. Sultans and slaves are the extremes. There are still many middle classes, up to the king and the true cynic—the class of consummate health. Terrorists and courtiers then fit in the class nearest after the sultans and slaves—and fit together like them. Both are representatives of both forms of sickness, indicative of a weak constitution.

The healthy constitution under a maximum of stimulation represents the king—the same under a minimum of excitation—the true cynic. The more alike both are, the more freely and constantly their roles can be exchanged, the nearer their constitution is to the perfect, completed constitution. The more independently a king dwells upon his throne, the more he is king.

All attractions are relative—are great—except one, which is absolute, and more than great.

The most complete constitution arises through the invocation of and absolute union with this Attraction. Through it one can dispense with the remainders—and then it begins to work vigorously, so that the relative attractions fall away and disappear. One has but one whole power, so one becomes wholly indifferent to the lesser, relative attractions. This Attraction is—absolute love.

A cynic and a king apart from this are only titles.

Each improvement of an incomplete constitution courses back upstream, in order that one is made more capable of love.

The best state endures from this kind of indifference.

In incompleted states there are still the best of citizens. Quick to mention all good qualities, they laugh silently over the tomfoolery of their contemporaries, and contain themselves concerning their evil. They don't seek to rectify error, because they know that each correction of this kind and under such premises is only a new error, and the Best cannot come from outside. They abandon all rank and title, and so are not troubled—and so they trouble no one and are everywhere welcome.[14]

113

New Fragments

As fragment the incomplete still appears most bearable—thus is this form of communication recommended to those still not wholly ready—and it does have individual, strange views to offer.
114

It is certain that everywhere the Highest, the Universal and the Obscure are at play, and that every inquiry soon hits upon dark and obscure thoughts.
115

Ere now, all was appearing as spirit. Now we see nothing but dead reiteration, which we don't understand. The meaning of hieroglyphics is absent. We still live upon the fruit of better times.
116

I. *Poeticism*

We are now only at the beginning of the writer's art.
117

Poetry dissolves foreign existences into itself.
118

Poetry is the true absolute Real. That is the kernel of my philosophy. The more poetic, the more true.
119

Genius is, after all poetic. Where genius has worked, it has poetically worked. The truly moral man is the poet.
120

Only an artist can divine the sense of life.
                121

Poetry is the great art of constructing transcendental health. Hence the poet is the transcendental physician.

Poetry rules and governs with pleasure and pain—with lust and aversion—error and truth—health and sickness—she mingles all to further her great aim of aims—the exaltation of man above himself.
                122

Poetry is generation. All compositions must be living individuals. What an inexhaustible amount of materials for new individual combinations lies all around us! Whoever has once divined these mysteries—he need do no more than renounce unending complexity with its mere pleasures and begin anywhere—but this very resolution costs us our free contact with the infinite world—and demands the confinement of infinity to an isolated phenomenon.

Should we perchance ascribe to analogous decisions our earthly presence?[15]
                123

The genuine poet is all-knowing—he is an actual world in miniature.
                124

The first man is the first spiritual seer. To him, all appears as spirit. What are children, if not such primal ones? The fresh insight of children is more boundless than the presentiments of the most resolute prophets.
                125

Nothing is more romantic than that which one ordinarily terms 'world' and 'fate.' —We live in a colossal novel. Observation of events around us here. Romantic orientation toward, estimation of, and approach to human life.

126

When one reads correctly, there unfolds then in our interior a real, visible world according to the words.

127

All novels where genuine love is presented are fairy-tales—magical events.

128

The lives of cultured people should alternate between music and non-music, as between sleep and waking.

129

The sorcerer is a poet. The prophet is to the sorcerer as the man of taste is to the poet.

130

The primal art is hieroglyphic.

131

Body, soul and spirit are the elements of the world—as epic, lyric and drama are the elements of poetry.

132

The lyric poem is for heroes; it makes heroes. The epic poem is for humanity. The hero is lyric, the human is epic, the genius is dramatic. Man is epic, woman is lyric, marriage is dramatic.

133

It would be a question ripe for inquiry: whether then the lyric poem would be inherently poetic—plus-poetry—or prose—minus-poetry? As prose has been determined for the novel, so the lyric poem has been fixed as poetry—but both preconceptions are wrong. The highest, purest prose is the lyric poem.

134

Whoever cannot create poetry will be only a fruitless, negative critic. To the true critic belongs the faculty of criticizing his own work. One who is only a poetaster judges fruitlessly.
135

Universal observation. On vignettes.[16] (All ashes are pollen—the calyx [chalice] is heaven.)
136

The repose[17] of the spirit realm is the flowering world. Humanity still slumbers in India, and its holy dream is a Garden, in which oceans of milk and sugar flow.
137

The sense for poetry has much in common with the sense for mysticism. It is the sense for the characteristic, the personal, the unknown, the mysterious, the manifest, the necessary accident. It describes the indescribable. It sees the invisible, feels the imperceptible, and so forth.
138

Poetry is for humanity what the chorus is for a Greek play—an attitude of the beautiful, rhythmic soul—the accompanying voice of our symbolic self—movement in the land of beauty—everywhere the faint trace of the fingers of humanity—free regulation—victory over raw nature in every word—whose wit is the expression of freer, more voluntary action—soaring—humanization—enlightenment—rhythm—art.
139

Art is the complement of nature.
140

The urgency of all artworks.
141

All that is perfect speaks not alone—it expresses a whole,

analogous world. There is suspended about each kind of perfection the veil of the eternal woman—which the lightest touch dissolves in magical vapors, and which proves to be the cloud-chariot of the seers. It is not antiquity alone that we see—she is in the heavens, the telescope—and the fixed star at once—and hence is a true revelation of the higher world.

Yet we shouldn't believe too rigidly that likewise the ancient and the perfected have been made—made in the usual sense of the word. For they are created just as the Beloved is created, by the arranged sign of the friend in the night—by the spark of the guide's touch—like the star in the eye. Exactly as the star shines through and penetrates the telescope—just so a heavenly form shines through the marble figure. (Poetic theory of the telescope—the star is a spontaneous light-hurler—the telescope or eye a receiver.)

With each aspect perfected, the work springs from the master into more than space, and so the master sees with the last stroke (of the brush) what is ostensibly his work,[18] separated from himself by a thought-fissure the breadth of which he hardly fathoms, and which only the power of the imagination, like the shadow of the soul's intelligence, is able to overcome. In the instant that the whole being should become alive, it is beyond him—he, its creator—he became an unknowing attribute and organ of a higher power.

The artist belongs to the work and not the work to the artist.

142

II. *Logological Fragments*

In the essential sense, philosophizing is—a caress—a testimony to the inner love of reflection, the absolute delight of wisdom.

143

In the world we search for a design—this design is we

ourselves. —What are we? Personifications, omnipotent points.
144

The world is, in any case, the result of a reciprocation between me and the Godhead. All that is—and arises—arises from the touch of the spirit.
145

The world will always, unendingly, be of the living—the conjoining of multiplicity can never end; the thinking I can never reach inertia. There are golden ages known to appear; but they don't bring an end to things—the aim of man is not the golden age. Rather, it is that he should eternally exist, be a beautiful, ordered individual, and abide—this is the tendency of his nature.
146

The known, to which the philosopher reduces all, and from whence he should proceed, must become the ur-known—the absolutely known. All consummation is ours naturally, and is known absolutely.
147

Philosophy must only make amends for the failures of our education—else we have no need of it.
148

The true philosophical act is the slaying of the self; this is the real beginning of all philosophy, therein lies the requirement for all philosophic youths, and only this act answers all criteria and conditions for the transcendental deed.
149

Our thought was until now either merely mechanistic—discursive—atomistic—or merely intuitive—dynamic. —Has now perchance the time of combination come?
150

Energy is the substance of matter.[19] Soul is the energy of energies. Spirit is the soul of souls. God is the spirit of spirits.
 151

Ecstasy[20] of procreation.—All procreation is also a polemic operation. Ecstasy of synthesis.
 152

I resemble not-I—the higher movement and principle of all art and knowledge.
 153

I am you.
 154

Instead of cosmogony and theogony, we busy our philosophers with anthropogony.
 155

Shemhamphorasch[21]—the Name of Names. The real definition is—a magic-word, a spell. Each idea has a scale of names—the supreme is absolute, and inexpressible. The names come to be in accordance with their common center, and reach at last in antithetic names beyond, from which the highest Naming arises anew.
 156

The greatest good endures in the imagination.
 157

Symbols are mystification.
 158

The consummate form of knowledge must be poetic. Each theorem must have an individual character—it must be a self-evident individuum, enveloping a flash of insight.
 159

The poetic philosopher is in the state of the absolute creator. A circle, a triangle are already in this respect created. But they have no attributes, save those the creator gives them.

One must above all always bear in mind that the highest—certainly not in an actual, but in an ideal poetic sense—comes before the low, the base. And even as the mathematician truly does something correctly, he does so as a philosophical poet.
160

Philosophy is essentially homesickness—the universal impulse to be home.
161

The world must become romanticized. So one finds the original sense renewed. Romanticization is nothing but a qualitative exponentiation. The lower self becomes identified with the better self in this operation. In the same way we ourselves are such a qualitative exponential series. This operation is still totally unknown. In it I give the common sense a higher sense, the quotidian a longing, homesick aspect, the familiar the majesty of the unfamiliar, the finite an infinite shine—hence I romanticize it. —The inverse is the operation for the higher, unfamiliar, mystic and infinite.—this becomes, through these combinations, logarithmic—it becomes a familiar expression. Romantic philosophy. Novel language. Lingua romana. Higher exchange and reduction.
162

Poetry is the champion of philosophy. Philosophy raises poetry to its fundamental principle. It teaches us to know the worth of poetry. Philosophy is the theory of poetry. It demonstrates to us that what poetry can be, one and all could be.
163

We will come to understand the world when we understand

ourselves, since we and it are integrating in the center. God's children, godly embryos are we. One day we are to become what our Father is.
>164

In intellectual vision is the key to life.
>164a

Transcendental poetry is an admixture of poetry and philosophy. It is fundamentally concerned with all transcendental functions, and in its activity, without question, contains the transcendent. The poet is, above all, the transcendental man.
>164b

III. *Sophie, or On Woman*

It is with love as with philosophy—she is and should be wholly each and everything. Love is also the I—the ideal of each aspiration.
>165

The heart is the key to the world and to life. One lives in this helpless condition in order to love and to meet other obligations. Through incompleteness one becomes susceptible to other influences, and to assimilate those strange influences is the aim. In sickness only should and can others help us. So Christ is, from this point of view, certainly, the key to the world.
>166

The need for love betrays a prior disunity within us. Need always betrays weakness.
>167

One is alone with whomever, whatever one loves.
>168

Love has from time immemorial been portrayed in romances—or the art of love has always been Romantic.

169

Whoever has much intellect in a certain sense, for him all becomes unique: his passion, his situations, his inclinations, the events around him—in short, everything he touches becomes absolute, becomes Fate.

170

Love is the design of universal history—the Amen of the universe.

171

The Christian religion is the characteristic religion of ecstasy. Sin is the great impulse for the love of the Godhead. The more wicked one perceives oneself, the more Christian one is. Unconditional union with the Godhead is the aim of sin and of love. Dithyrambs are a genuine Christian product.

172

The dithyramb, in its physical action, is an embrace. It must, therefore, be judged according to natural law.

173

Plato made love a child of the destitute, of the impulsive—and of the excessive.

174

Guilt and ignorance are sisters. However, there are noble and common sisters. Common guilt and ignorance are mortal—each is a pretty little sister, but without meaning and not enduring. The noble sisters are immortal: their high form is unchanging, and their countenances are eternally lit by the days of paradise. Both live in heaven and seek only noble and tested human beings.

175

All enchantment is an artistic madness. All passion is an enchantment. An alluring maiden is an actual sorceress, inasmuch as one believes in her.
176

All enchantment takes place through the partial identification with the enchanted—through it I can compel a subject to see, to trust, to feel just as I do.
177

The everyday life is a priestly service—almost a vestal one. We are engaged with nothing so much as with the preservation of the holy and mysterious flame—a duplicate, as it appears. The extent to which we foster and keep it depends upon us. Should the nature of our care be perchance the measure of our truth, our love, and our solicitude for the highest character of our essence? True calling—symbolic evidence of our religiosity, of our essence? (Fire-worshipper).
178

There is only one temple in the world, and that is the human body. Nothing is holier than this high Form.
One touches heaven, when one touches a human body.[22]
Beyond the killing of the old, the crippled and the ailing.
179

A character is a completed, refined Intention.
180

Inclinations to master oneself are more praiseworthy than inclinations to flee.
181

Woman is the symbol of good and beauty; man is the symbol of truth and right.
182

Shouldn't it speak for the superiority of the woman's circumstances, that the extremes she generates are greater than our own? The most degenerate man is not as different from the respectable one as the most miserable excuse for a woman differs from the most noble one. Have they not similarity with the Infinite, in that they find fulfillment not in manipulation of the outer world, but in nurture?[23] And so it is with the highest, that which is unconditionally near us, and yet always sought, that which is absolute understanding, and yet which we don't understand, that which is indispensable, and yet for the most part dispensed with. And so it is with the loftiest Being, that which appears so childlike, so commonplace, so superfluous and so playful—

Even their greater helplessness exalts them over us, as does their greater independence, their greater slavery, their greater despotism; and so they are therefore over us and under us and yet they are more coherent and indivisible than we.

Would we even love, were this not so? With woman arose love, and with love woman arises, and therefore one can't be understood without the other.
183

They are a lovely mystery—only veiled, not locked up. In an analogous way the philosopher's mystery attracts us. Hetaerae.[24] Their soul-power. Gaze upon the hereafter. The act of embracing—the Greek Goddesses. Madonna. Each people, each time have their lovely woman-symbol. Women in poetry. To the lover she is the ultimate reality. On the feminine season. Only woman and love dissolve the intellect.
184

Marriage is the highest mystery. Marriage is, for us, a popularized secret. A pity that there is, for us, only a choice between marriage and solitude. Extreme it is,—but how few people are capable of a genuine marriage—and how few can even endure solitude. There, in marriage, is the union of all kinds. Marriage is an unending union. —Isn't woman the aim of man,

and is woman without a like aim?
185

Marriage signifies a new, higher epoch of love—the companion—the compulsory love—the living love. Philosophy originates with marriage.
186

Gaming is the ground of all patriotism.
187

Each wrong deed, each unworthy sentiment, is an infidelity to the Beloved—an adultery.
188

Rightly can many a woman say that she *sinks* into the arms of her lover. —Wealth to those who into their lover's arms, *rise*.
189

Woman knows how to sustain man, and man knows how to sustain woman upon the most natural good.
190

Clothing must be autonomous—free, creating beauty of itself—congruent.[25]
191

Self-judgement follows after actual events—after the purely external aspects, not after the inner weaving and significance. How much more lovely is the skin of bodies than that loathsome inner essence!
192

Love can only transcend through the absolute religious will. One realizes the highest essence only through death. (Death-reconciliation.)
193

All absolute sensation is religious.
                    194

All our inclinations appear to be nothing but applied religion. The heart appears to be identical with the religious organ. Perhaps the higher offspring of the productive hearts are—none other than heaven. While the heart is abstracted from all individual actual subjects—one finds oneself, one makes of oneself an idealized subject, and religion originates. All individual inclinations coalesce into one—of whose wonderful object—a higher essence, a Godhead is—hence genuine God-fear embraces all sensation and inclination. This natural God eats with us, gives birth to us, speaks with us, sleeps with us, lets itself eat in us, procreate in us, and is born in us; in brief—the natural God is the infinite substance of our activity and our suffering.

We make the Beloved into such a God: in this is practical religion.
                    195

In humanity must one seek God. In human concerns, in human thoughts and sensations is the spirit of heaven revealed most brightly.

Religious learning is wholly separated from these. But only thus can it be understandable and useful to religious humanity.

One cannot proclaim religion as other than love and patriotism. When one wishes to make love to someone, how does one best begin?
                    196

The smaller and slower one begins—the more perfect the result—and this is true everywhere. The more one can do with a few—the more one can do with many.[26] When one understands how to love one—then one understands even better how to love all.

Art: to transmute everything in Sophia—or vice versa.
                    197

Soul-magnet.
197a

Adam and Eve. What through a revolution was effected, must through a revolution be overthrown. (Apple-bite).
197b

IV. *Notes on the Margin of Life*

To become human is an art.
198

Each thinking man will of course find Truth—he may then proceed where and go just as he will.
199

To be the more complete human—person—that is the destiny and the primal (*ur-*) impulse in humanity.
200

Each person that overcomes his persona is a person in two powers—or a genius. In this respect, one can truly say that there were no Greeks, but rather those who had been given Greek genius. An educated Greek was only very indirectly, and so a small component of, his adopted work. Hence the greater (and purer) individuality of the Greek arts and sciences—which one can scarcely deny—is accounted for by the fact that within limits they had seized upon and modernized Egyptian and Oriental mysticism. In Ionia one marks the softening influx of the warmer Asiatic heavens, just as on the other hand one will perceive in the early Doric people the mysterious hardness and strangeness of the Egyptian Godhead. Later writers have often noted these ancient forms of modern and romantic instinct, and observed that native forms may be inspired with new spirit, and placed among modern people in order to contain the thoughtless

course of modern civilization and to turn their attention back to abandoned holy places.
201

How little people have cultivated multiplicity—have cultivated silent total watchfulness of all which is in and about them, in each instant educated. Bonnet's observation: Watchfulness is the mother of genius.
202

With instinct man comes, within instinct man is bound to end. Instinct is the genius in paradise—for the period of self-separation (self-knowledge).[27]
203

All must become nourishment. Art is to distill life from everything. To enliven all is the aim of life. *Lust* (delight) is life. Unlust (aversion) is the remedy for delight, just as death is the remedy for life.
204

Just as nothing can be free, so also nothing can be mastered, save spirit. In addition, only a spirit constrains. Thus whatever constrains itself, is a spirit—insofar as it masters itself.
205

Bias and attachment are for the imagination what fog, blinding light, and colored spectacles are for the eyes.
206

Through far too copious reflection upon himself, man became blunted and forfeited a healthy sense of himself.
207

Annihilation of the lower needs. Only through needs am I limited—or limitable. One must will the lower needs, and all that which one cannot make voluntary[28] as absolutely unavailable, as non-existent. Thereby am I exalted by all associations with them.

208

We know only insofar as we make.

209

Something which inhibits our free action becomes ours only if we take it up in the inner sphere through our free action—thus we also feel pain and are yet independent of it. One must come to receive even the greatest misfortune in this sphere, if suffering is to truly affect us—else it remains foreign to and outside us.

210

Whether you conform with things, or things conform with you is immaterial, is one.

211

Freedom is like luck—that detrimental, and that useful.

212

Where one places one's reality, where one fixes it: that is one's God, one's world, one's all. Relativity of morality.

213

The higher something is, the less it overturns—rather, the more it strengthens and corrects.

214

Only the lasting is worth our whole attention—the permanently useful.

215

To learn something is a very beautiful pleasure—and to know something real is the source of that delightfulness.

216

It is not knowledge alone that makes us successful—it is the quality of the knowledge, the subjective nature of the knowledge. Consummate knowledge is conviction, and it is this which makes us successful and gratifies us.
217

From how few peoples is a history possible! A people gain their preferences through literature and artworks, and what else remains from the individual, characteristic residuum? It is natural that a people first become historical when they become a public. Is then man historical, until he comes of age, and a suitable Reality steps forth?
218

Mystic truth and devotion to the ancient and familiar which once was—and mystic hope and delight in all which should come—the new and unfamiliar—these are the two most important characteristics of the human race until now.
219

Soldiers have colorful clothing because they are the blood of the state, worldly enthusiasts. Oxide. The spiritual are pure carbon—throughout burning, light-concentrating, binding Nature, warming and glowing. Great affinity for oxygen.
220

To what extent can we never attain the Ideal? Insofar as the Ideal would annihilate itself. In order to perform the working of the Ideal, don't permit the self to stay in the sphere of ordinary reality. I gain nobility in freer elevation above myself—consequently I can, in certain respects, never be absolutely exalted—for otherwise I would become its agent, its delight, its triumph. In brief, I myself would cease to be. Vice is a perpetually increasing torment (negation) and a feeling of involuntarily descending (unconsciousness)—Virtue is perpetually increasing delight—position—a feeling of power—ascendance from the accidental.

So it is with the wicked, who because of their proximity to opportunity can mistake, can fail to be virtuous—while the virtuous are never near the opportunity to err. The quantity or the duration is no measure of its worth—the victory that the wicked of the thousandth grade under zero win over themselves is so much more than the triumph that the virtuous of the thousandth grade over null win by fighting. The space or the time that divides them can in an instant be flown past—for there are here no quantitative relations or conditions. There are two absolutely separate spheres, which we but posit as quantitative, and imagine each victory and each defeat as steps forward and backward.[29]

Custom is lightening for the good and impeding for the bad—and herein lie the long and the short of it—the longer the miscreant's punishment, the longer the reward for the virtuous.
221

Wishes and desires are flight—there are wishes and desires that conform so little to earthly conditions that we certainly could end in a state, from too mighty a swing, in which we rise to an element or lower ourselves to an island.[30]
222

One can always concede that man has a predominant bent toward evil—the better he is by nature, the less the dissimilar attracts.
223

Even chance is not unfathomable—it has its regularity.
224

Play is experimenting with chance.
225

Whoever has the right sense for chance can employ everything conditional to determine unknown possibilities—he can

see destiny with the same luck in the positions of stars as in grains of sand, in the flights of birds, and in figures and images.
226

All chance is wonderful—touching upon higher essences—a problem, data for the active religious senses.
227

Slumber is the cessation of the higher organs—a withdrawal of the spiritual impulses—the higher organs are absolutely bound to these impulses. The free will is hemmed in, circumscribed. —Sleep, the analogue of death. Briefer, but more often—sleep. Its restorative effect. It is a sign that when one sleeps well, one is proportionately wide awake afterward. As one requires less sleep, the more is one complete. An eyeblink's intermission fortifies nearly more than a longer one. Half-consciousness in sleep. The singular dream-builder. The dream of life. (Time blurs the subjects into one another. Each view of the future fully invigorates; manifold life is in a morning's prospects. Poetic curve of the sun. Life ends with the day, a completed drama—melancholy—but with an exalted hope. The evening is sentimental, as the morning is naive. The morning must be austere and active, the evening abundant. Likewise, one must work toward midday, while toward evening, and dinner, work abates again. In the morning there is no companionship. One is young in the morning and old in the evening. Each evening we must find our will and our affairs in order.)
228

Many feel the approach of the spirit's presence—therefore they have that much more spiritual future.
229

One should feel proud of sorrow and pain—each sorrow, each pain, is an attainment of a higher rank.
230

Martyrs are spiritual heroes. Each man has his own day of martyrdom. Christ was the great martyr of our race. Through him is martyrdom unendingly deep and holy. O—that I could have a martyr's sense!
231

Should the devil, as father of the lie, be himself only a necessary ghost? Deception and illusion stand alone against truth, purity and religion.

The free will stands against capriciousness, slavishness, moodiness, superstition, perversity, all of which work through pure chance, by way of a given intentionality. Here arises the deception.

To God there is no devil—but for us he is unfortunately a very effective chimera. Realm of the demonic.

Obligation: to be serene, calm.
232

Many a deed haunts you forever.
233

We are here outside the time of the universally valid Forms.[31]
234

Apparently we go forward.
235

For God we actually go inversely.
From older to younger.
236

Death is the romanticizing principle of our life. Death is a minus; life is a plus. —Through death, life is laid bare.
237

Everything excellent merits ostracism. It is good that this is so, since excellence exists through ostracism. Everything absolute must be ostracized from the world. In the world, one must live with the world. One only lives in a human sense, when one lives in the manner of the people around one. All that is good in the world comes from here within (and thus passes from here outward), but it only flashes like lightning, briefly. The excellent ones bring the world forward, but their work is quickly over.
238

When we see a giant, we inquire after the sun's position, and pay attention, to see if it isn't only a pygmy's shadow.
(On the colossal workings of the small—aren't they all clearly like the shadows of pygmies?)
239

V. *From the Hidden World*

All that is visible rests upon the invisible—the audible upon the inaudible—the felt upon the unfelt. Perhaps thinking rests upon unthinking.
240

Could light be but the sign of the new union—the visible Genius of union together? . . .
241

Light is the vehicle of the world's communion; is this true community not likewise in the spiritual sphere?
242

Light is the symbol of true presence of mind. Hence the analogy: light is the means of matter's self-reference. Day is the consciousness of the planet, and in the Sun's reign, like a god inspired by the eternal spontaneity of the center, does one planet turn in accord with the others, opening its eye and awakening for a longer or shorter time, and then renewing itself in the coolness of sleep, awaiting new life and new contemplation. Thus even here there is religion—for is the life of the planet something other than sun-worship? Even here you come to answer us with the primeval childlike religion of the Parsee,[32] and in it, in you, we find the religion of the cosmos.

243

What then is the sun? One through whom we receive stimulation, within whom we always find self-reference, an eternally luminous body. And a planet? A relative excitation, for strange stimuli harmonize the body.[33]

244

Humanity is in the highest sense our planets; the nerves are those members linked with the superior world; the eyes are that which one raises toward heaven.

245

Man is a Sun and his senses are planets.

246

Inner and outer vastnesses, unending All...

247

Light is in any case action—light is like life, the effecting force—one only in the coinciding conditions of revelation. Light causes fire. Light is the genius of the fire-processes. Life is like light, in its waxing and waning, and in its gradual negation. Doesn't life also, like light, break up into colors? The process of nutrition is not a cause, but rather a result of life.

All effecting is transformation. In chemistry one observes things changing one into another. But this is not so in that which one terms mechanical influence.

Sign of sickness: the instinct for self-destruction. Thus is everything incomplete—so life itself—or better, the organic stuff of life.

Dissolution of the differences between life and death. Annihilation of death.
248

Light is the action of the cosmos—the eye is the superior means of sensing the cosmos—or world-soul—world-action. Rays, therefore, are simply a fiction.
249

Humanity is in relation to the moral sense as sound and light are to the ear and to the eye.
250

Silence favors weight and coherence—slowness brings about the opposite of rapidity. Each transparent body is in a higher condition—it appears to have a kind of consciousness.
Sleep appears to be a penetration of the inorganic world into the organic.
251

Philosophical Instructions for the Experimenter.
Could the flame, the spark, be part of a new realm, distinct from the plant, the animal and the human kingdoms? Living processes.
Four varieties of the flame— 1. The hereafter, of whose detritus—inorganic nature is; 2. of whose detritus—plants are; 3. of whose detritus—-animals are; 4. of whose detritus—humanity is. The higher the flame, the more artificial—the more complex the creation of excrement. All devouring is an assimilation-process—a binding-together—a generation-process. The flame is voracious.
Fermentation—even excrement has a flame-nature. The flame devours even yet, as one sees in rusting metal.
252

The tree can only come to be according to the blossoming flame—people can only come to be according to the speaking

flame—and animals can only come to be according to the changing flame.
253

All spiritual touching is the same as the touch of a magician's wand. Everything can become magical-work. But whoever brings forth such a marvelous touch's effect, whoever brings forth the magical incantation's effect, he remembers only the first touch of the Beloved's hand, in that first meaningful moment in which the magic-wand breaks the light's ray, the first kiss, the first word of love—and asks himself, whether the spell and the magic of this moment is not also marvelous and wonderful, indissoluble and eternal.
254

Charcoal and diamond are one substance, and yet are different! Could there not be a similar relationship between man and woman? We are the clay and women are world-eyes and sapphires, which likewise consist of clay.
255

All is seed.
256

Our spirit is a connecting link to the wholly incomparable.
257

Nothing is more attainable to the spirit than the infinite.
258

In the end, the comprehensibility of phenomena rests upon faith and will. If I make a mystery of a manifestation, then it is a mystery for me. It is therefore the same with boundaries.[34]
259

We should not be merely human; we should be even more than human. —Humanity is, after all, greater than the universe.

Humanity is not bound. —Man can and should be bound and unbound at once.
260

Man isn't drawn alone to a given science; man must be human—through his humanity is his decision determined, universal tendencies being indispensable to any individual talent. But man must never seek an ideal like a phantast seeking something indeterminate, a child of phantasy. He should rather go from specific attempt to specific attempt. An unknown beloved has a magical fascination. But striving after the unknown or undetermined is extremely dangerous and disadvantageous. Revelation authorizes nothing demanding violence.
261

The world is a universal trope of the spirit, a symbolic image therefrom.
262

What is man? A consummate trope of the spirit. All true communication is also sensory imagery—and so aren't the lover's caresses the highest communication?
263

Through man the human world will be conjoined, as the body's components are conjoined through their life.
264

Living energy—indirect invention—wonder-energy.
Cloud's play—nature-play's uttermost poetic. Nature is an Aeolian harp—she is a musical instrument—whose notes are sounding anew higher chords within us. (Idea-association).
265

Universal, inner, harmonious coherence is simply that

which should be.
266

The idea of our infinite freedom involves an unending progression from our manifestation in the sensory world. We will not be bound by this singular manifestation in our earthly bodies upon this planet.
267

Must then all humans be human? There is still a whole other Reality, other than the human in humanlike form.
268

When the spirit perishes, it becomes human. When the human perishes, it becomes spirit. Death frees the spirit, death frees the human.
What corresponds to the human existence hereafter?
The daemonic—or the existence of the Genius—to whom the body is that which the soul is to us.[35]
269

Ritter's view of the beginning and the disappearance of matter sheds light on death. —Who knows where we, in an instant, might crystallize? In that instant here we disappear. Must there then be on all worlds a similar procreation? —The Sun's influence makes it very plausible that the Sun could be known wherever we might find ourselves.[36]
270

The more the opposition, the greater the love—an absolute opposition creates an absolute love. To you I return, noble Kepler, whose higher sense of an inspirited, ethical world was exhausted, so that rather in our times this be held for wisdom—to kill everything, to degrade the highest, to raise up the vile, and to place the human spirit under the law of mechanism.
271

Our body is a component of the world—limb is better put. Our autonomy must be understood through this analogy of the whole—in short, through the conception of the microcosmos. These limbs must correspond to the whole. So many senses: so many modes of the universe. —The spirit is utterly analogous to the human essence in body, soul and spirit. The first abbreviates, the second elongates the same substance.
272

The blossom is the symbol of our spirit's secrets.
273

Infinite distance of the blossoming world.
274

Tolerance and cosmopolitanism of the flowers. They strive after the individual, undivided sovereignty of the animal.
275

The moral system must become a natural system. All sickness is the equivalent of sin; it is through an excess that it is transcended. Our sicknesses are all phenomena of a heightened sensation that in greater force will overflow. As man would become God, he sins. —The sickness of plants is animalization; the sickness of animals is rationalization; the sickness of stones is vegetation. Shouldn't each plant correspond to a stone and to an animal?[37] Reality of sympathy. Parallelisms of the natural realm. —Plants are dead stones; animals are dead plants, and so forth. Theory of metempsychosis.
276

The heaven-body makes a fourth realm, under the stones.[38]
277

Could the world be petrification? Perhaps from Angels.[39]
278

We can only become acquainted with Creation as His work insofar as we ourselves are God. We know it not insofar as we ourselves are of the world. Knowledge is increasing—when we become more God. Does God know himself?
279

Each voluntarily or randomly chosen individual can become a world-organ for us. A glance, a star, a region, an ancient tree can in our interior create epochs. This is the great reality of fetishism, of idolatry.
280

Seasons, days, life and fate are all, strangely enough, throughout rhythmical, metrical, measured. In all handwork, in all art, in all machines, in organic bodies, in all our daily work, everywhere: rhythm, meter, beat, melody. Everything that we do with any certainty, we do with an unobserved rhythm. Rhythm one finds everywhere; it insinuates itself everywhere. All mechanisms are metrical, rhythmic. And here yet more lies: should it be merely the influence of laziness?
281

Nerves are the higher root of the senses.
282

The division into the five senses is wholly incorrect.
Our senses are five animals. From them arises an even higher Animalism.
283

Plants work from the human plant-sense, animals from the human animal-sense, stones from the human stone-sense.
284

Trees appear the most exalted among all plants, because they fasten so many intermediate, innumerable individuals to the earth, and because they are as if they were already plants above plants.

The senses are to animals what leaves and flowers are to plants. Flowers are allegories of consciousness, or of minds, heads. A higher propagation is the aim of the higher flower, a higher preservation: in the human consciousness there is also an organ of immortality, its aim a progressive propagation of the personality. Remarkable inferences and conclusions for both realms.

285

On the time when birds, animals and trees have speech.[40]

286

The animal lives among animals, in the air. —Plants are half-animal, and therefore live part in the earth and, the greater plants, with part of themselves in the air. —Earth is the greatest means of sustenance for air. Air, breath, is Brahman. The conjoining of Nitrogen and Oxygen in the air is everywhere not merely a chemical, but an animal process.

287

As only the eye sees eyes, so understanding is only known through understanding—the soul through the soul—intelligence through intelligence—spirit through spirit—and so forth—imagination only through imagination—the senses only through the senses—and God can only be known to God.

288

Every word is a word of incantation. Whatever spirit is called, such a one appears.

289

Since God was able to become man, he can become even stones, plants, animals and elements, and perhaps there is in this way a perpetual deliverance in nature.

Individuality in nature is wholly infinite.
How much does this prospect, our hopes for a universal personality invigorate us!
Is this not what the ancients called sympathy?
Even our thoughts are effective factors of the universe.
290

Satan and God are the extremes, between which stands man. The devil is the negating, God the creating power.
291

Madness and magic have many similarities. A magician is an artist of madnesses.
292

Could wonder effect conviction? Or wouldn't the true conviction, the highest function of our heart and our personality, herald the unique, true Godly wonder? Each wonder unlinked with our higher consciousness must remain isolated in us, a dream. But an inner, moral conviction, a Godly vision, that would be a true, sustained conviction.
293

The greatest magician would be him who could so conjure as to make his conjuration a self-empowered, estranged manifestation. Could this not be the case with each of us?
294

The true historical sense is the prophetic vision-sense—which clearly arises from the innermost infinite conjunction of the whole world.
295

Realization—the reflection and experimentation of God is the true source of life.
296

Dream of the future—is a thousand-year reign possible? One day when all vice is to be exiled? When understanding is matured, completed.
297

Judgement day is the synthesis of present lives and deaths (deaths according to lives).
298

Instruction for life in the hereafter. Our life is no dream—but it should and perchance will become one.
299

The Encyclopedia

The sciences are only separate out of a deficiency of genius and discernment—the relationships between them are too involved for the intellect and for common sense—and thereby they eliminate one another.

For the greatest truths of our day, we are indebted to combinations of the long separated aspects of total knowledge.
    300

Partial histories are thoroughly impossible—each history must be a world-history, and only in relation to the whole history is the historical treatment of a particular situation possible.
    301

Contemplation of the larger and contemplation of the smaller must occur together—that one become manifold, this one become simple. Not only the composite data of the world's structure, but even the individual components thereof (macrocosm and microcosm) magnify and augment one another through reversed analogies. —So the whole clarifies the part, and the part clarifies the whole.
    302

My knowledge will become a kind of scientific grammar—or logic—or, as in music, the underlying bass-tone—an instruction for composition—with examples.
    303

Everyone should endorse an encyclopedia. All fundamental knowledge ultimately becomes neglected.
    304

My book should become a scientific Bible—a real and ideal paragon—and a seed of all books.
305

Shouldn't the Bible be understood as still developing? The Biblical utterances are infinitely variegated—History, poetry, all in profusion.—
306

Knowledge is only one half. Faith is the other.
307

Each science has its God, together with its objective. Hence lives the unique mechanism of the *perpetuum mobili*—and thus, to construct a *perpetuum mobili*, one seeks to equal time itself as one's highest problem. And thus chemistry seeks the *menstruo universali*—and the spiritual substance, or philosopher's stone. Philosophy seeks a primal and unique principle. The mathematician searches for the quadrature of the circle, and a similar principle. Man—God. The medicinal elixir of life—an essence of youth and the consummate feeling for and use of the body. The politics of the consummate state—eternal harmony—a freed state.

It is due only to the deficient nature, to the incompleted relationships of the various elements which comprise this enquiry, that it hasn't been solved. The problems are theoretically real, and identically composed: so, for instance, perpetual motion, eternal life and the squared circle. Philosophy of these enquiries.
308

Paradise is strewn over the earth—and therein become unknown—its scattered lineaments are bound to coalesce—its skeleton is bound to become enfleshed. Regeneration of paradise.
309

The schema of the ideal humanity and its knowledge is likewise the central schema of all scientific and practical and artistic criticism.

The artist is the synthesis of the theoretician and the practitioner.

310

Everything which a learned one does, says, speaks, endures, hears, and so forth, must be an artistic, technical, scientific product, or operation. He speaks in epigrams, he acts in a drama, he speaks in dialogues, he bears treatises and knowledge—he relates anecdotes, histories, fairy-tales, novels, and experiences life poetically; when he signs something, he signs it as an artist, as a musician; his life is a novel—and so he sees and hears everything—and so he reads.

In short, the truly learned one is a wholly refined human being—all that he touches upon and does, he gives a knowledgeable, idealistic, syncretic Form.

311

Just as Copernicus did, so all good researchers—physicians and observers and thinkers do—must do: turn the data and the method about, in order to see whether it wouldn't fit better that way.

312

We owe all the greatest truths of our day to contact with the long-separated limbs of total-knowledge.[41]

313

If our corporeal life is a burning to ashes, so doubtless our spiritual life is also a combustion. Thus is death perhaps a transformation of capacity.

314

There is no true distinction between *theoria* and *praxis*.

315

To search after originality is a more learned, yet crude egotism. Whoever doesn't treat each strange thought as his own, and each of his own thoughts as an alien thought, is no true scholar.

The generation of new ideas can become a useless luxury—true learning is an active accumulation—the cultivation of accumulation is already a higher grade of activity. For the true scholar there is nothing familiar and nothing strange. All is familiar and alien at once to him. (The philosophical body is itself both alien and familiar, alluring and irritating, together.)
316

The learned know how to appropriate the alien, and how to make the familiar strange. (To learn and to instruct—to observe and to describe—to digest and to secrete.)

Higher striving after a higher originality. —Even in the learned world one must love and choose, in order to exist, and know how to nourish, how to enjoy oneself.
317

A young scholar must begin with a special critique. From strange threads and fabrics he learns to set out particular ideas, and to spin out complete, well-fashioned weavings.
318

Reason and imagination are religion—reason and understanding are science.
319

I. *Philosophy*

To think is to speak. To speak and to do or to make are only modifications of the same operation. God spoke, and it was light, and it was.
320

Contrasts are inverse analogies.
321

To annihilate the principle of contradiction is perhaps the highest principle of the higher logic.
322

A gifted, systematizing man hears all ideas, all observations. He acquires them—he makes them his own through formation and use.
323

Spirit is a purified act.
324

Man has always understood philosophy as only a higher potential for knowledge in general—not specifically.
325

Philosophy is only a three-fold or doubled wakening—awakeness—consciousness.
326

The unknown, the mysterious, is the result and the beginning of all. (We only know intrinsically how to know ourselves.) Successions therefrom. Whatever is left to be comprehended is in an incomplete condition—it should gradually be made comprehensible. The conception or the knowledge is the prose—the indifferent. On both sides is a plus and a minus. Cognition is a way to attain anew lost knowledge. (Life instinct.) Nature is incomprehensible as such. Serene and cultivated incomprehension. Philosophy is prose. They are consonant. Distant philosophy rings like poetry—while each silence in the distance becomes vocal. On both sides, or nearby, lies plus and minus poetry. So everything at a distance becomes poetic—poetry acts in the distance. Distant mountains, distant people, distant ventures all become romantic, *quod idem est*—hence we devote our most poetic nature. Poetry of the night and of twilight.

The useful is, as such, prosaic. Each specific aim is, in general, a consonant, a restrained aim. Distant aim.

327

Every unbound, universal theme has something musical about it. It inspires philosophical fantasy—to express any given individual philosophical idea without a specific philosophical train of thought.

328

Philosophy is, like all synthetic sciences, like mathematics—voluntary. It is an ideal self-grounded method of observing the inner, and of ordering it. Hence could the philosophy of the unattainable be the scientific method?

329

The idea of philosophy is a mysterious tradition. Philosophy is above all the attempt to know. It is an indefinable science of the sciences—above all, a mysticism of wisdom's germinating impulse—like the spirit of knowledge—consequently unportrayable—save in an image or in an application, in the completed manifestation of a particular knowledge.

Now all wisdom is indivisible—therefore philosophy will never be consummated. Only in the complete system, which encompasses all sciences, will philosophy truly be visible. From this mystic property of philosophy it is clear why each seeks something else in philosophy, and that the true philosophy can never be illustrated.[42]

330

Philosophy can bake no bread—but it can secure us with God, freedom, and immortality—which is only practical.

Philosophy or economy?

331

It is dogmatic if I say—there is no God; there is no not-I; there is no thing-in-itself;[43] I can only speak critically; now there is, for me, no essence outside the imagination. All illusion is as essential as truth, just as the body is essential to the soul. Error is the indispensable instrument of truth. With error I make truth—the complete employment of error—the complete possession of truth.

All synthesis—all progression—or beginning to overcome illusion—arises from seeing outside me what is in me. I have faith and it comes to pass. Errors of time and space.[44]

To believe is to operate in the illusory—it is based in illusion. All knowledge in the distance is faith—the idea of that outside me is the thing itself. All knowledge begins and ends in faith. The expansion of knowledge, forward and backward, is the expansion of faith's domain. The I believes that it will see a strange being—and through approximation arises another, mediate essence—the product—to which I belong and, at the same time, to which I don't appear to belong. The mean result of these processes is the most important thing—that having appeared through chance—or in other words, the created thing is transformed intentionality.[45]
332

All barriers are only there for the traversing, and so forth.
333

Astronomy is the real algebra of physics—one could even call astronomy the metaphysics of nature.

Metaphysics and astronomy are one science. The Sun is, in astronomy, what God is in metaphysics. Freedom and immortality are light and warmth. God, freedom and immortality will one day prove the basis of a spiritual physics—as sun, light and heat are the basis of earthly physics.
334

Completed speculation leads back to nature.
335

Whoever knows what philosophizing is, knows what life is—and the inverse.
336

All can become experiment—all can become an organ. True practical knowledge arises from genuine experimentation. Fichte teaches the secrets of experimentation—he teaches data and deeds, or real facts and real acts, and in experiment and in perception he transmutes them. Data is comprehended in contrast to fact. The ideas are attached together—the action and the facts depend together—and all four are attached, in contradiction, together.

Fichte teaches us how to construct these four things and thus how to conjoin them—and he teaches their passing away.
337

Through experimentation we learn to observe. In experimentation we observe ourselves—and learn thereby to draw inferences from strange phenomena by reference to their unity—or by proper observance. In proper observation there is, moreover, already clarity.
338

Fichte's I is reason—his God and Spinoza's God have great similarities. God is the supersensible world, unalloyed—we are the diluted products thereof. We think our God is personal, just as we think ourselves personal. God is exactly as personal as we are—then our so-called I is not our true I, but rather only our reflection.
339

On the extraordinary degree of evidence, calm and cheerfulness that idealistic sentences (beautiful, faithful sentences) have: i.e.—'Everything that happens, happens for the best.'
340

All faith is wonderful and miraculous. God is in this instant, as I trust in Him. Faith is, indirectly, a wonderful power. Through faith we can, in each instant, perform miracles for ourselves—often for others as well, when they trust with us.

Faith here below is truly received as effect and sensation in another world—an interworldly celebration.[46] Genuine faith manifests each thing in another world. Faith is the experience of awakening and working and sensing in another world.

341

Plotinus was already, in regard to most experimental results, a critical idealist and realist. Fichte's and Kant's methods are still not complete and not sufficiently supported. Both still don't know how to experiment with facility and diversity—they are not poetic. Everything is so stiff, so anxious yet.

342

Don't even God and nature play? Theory of the players. Holy play.

343

Only here does absolute death become absolute greatness—which never is permitted to attain an ultimate reality—but absolute death contains the possibility of absolute life. Death is polar—life is thoroughly synthetic. From the interpenetration of plus and minus deaths arises life. Death is simple—elemental. The absolutely polarized elements in the interpenetration constitute absolute life. Incomplete elements, plus and minus elements, constitute only an incomplete life—although they are not fully realized, they can pierce through to know, but cannot realize a completed state of harmony.

The completed life is heaven. The world is the embodiment of incompleted lives. The supra-sensory harmony is the substance of life—as is the completed life—the world is an aggregate of accidents.[47] What we here name death is a succession of absolute lives, of heavens—therefore the perpetual destruction of all incomplete lives—these are incessantly digested, perpetual images of newer destruction—points, newer maws—these constantly eating and making absolute life—absolute joy. Each of these shall become heaven.[48]

344

Our thought is simply a galvanization—a touch of the earthly spirits—the spiritual atmosphere—through a heavenly unearthly spirit. All thinking is thus already a sympraxis in a higher world.

345

The higher philosophy deals with the marriage of nature and spirit.

346

II. *Mathematics and Natural Knowledge*

All historical knowledge strives to become mathematical. The mathematical power is an ordering power. Each mathematical science strives to become philosophical anew—to become animated or rationalized—then poetic—finally moral—ultimately religious.

347

Ultimately, the whole of mathematics is not a specific science—but rather only a general scientific tool. . . It is perhaps nothing other than the exoterizing of the soul's power to understand an external object—a realized and objectivized understanding. Should this not be the case with more and perhaps all soul-powers—that through our troubles such powers become external tools? Everything should become visible without us—our soul should be representable. —The system of the sciences should become a symbolical body (organ-system) of our inner world. — Our spirit should become a sensual and percipient machine—not

in us, but outside us.
348

The number system is the model of a true symbolic language. Our letters should become numbers, our language arithmetic.
What did the Pythagoreans truly mean by the powers of numbers?
349

Poetry of mathematics. Grammar of mathematics. Physics of mathematics. Philosophy of mathematics. History of mathematics. Mathematics of philosophy. Mathematics of nature. Mathematics of poetry. Mathematics of history. Mathematics of mathematics.
350

The complete mathematics is properly a grand equation for the other forms of knowledge.
All forms of knowledge are accordingly in debt to mathematics' existence. Pure mathematics is the inherent element of magicians.
In music it appears clearly as revelation—as creative idealism.
Here it is legitimized as a heavenly messenger, as anthropos.
The highest life is mathematical.
Pure mathematics is religion.
One only attains mathematics through a theophany.
In the East the pure mathematics is at home.
In Europe it is only destitute, a mere technical scrap. Whoever produces a mathematical book without devotion and without realizing God's Word in it understands it not.
Each line is a world-axis.
351

The highest and the purest is the mundane, the most under-

standable. Therefore elementary geometry is higher than higher geometry. The more difficult and intricate a science becomes, the more derivative, impure and adulterated it is.
352

It is very possible that even in nature marvellous mystic numbers occur. Even in history— Isn't everything full of meaning, symmetry, allusion, and strange relationships? Can't God reveal himself in mathematics, just as in every other form of knowledge?
353

Whoever in the first place understands how to count to two, sees, if he were to count still more, without doubt the possibility of an infinite counting following the same laws.
354

Remarkable, mysterious numbers. When numbers were still new, they must have come forth effectively as things—characteristic, enduring numbers like the ten fingers, for instance—and other striking numerical phenomena from the liveliest employment of the human imagination. And the ancients in their knowledge of numbers employed the profound and occult wealth of wisdom—a key to all the sealed doors of nature now relinquished, as punishment.
355

Crooked, circuitous lines—the triumph of free nature over rules.
356

Could all differences be only quantitative? Self between God and me. Absoluteness of mathematics.
357

Eternity is the sum, the extrapolation of time.
358

Physics is nothing but the teaching of the imagination.
359

As it went with the ancients, so it goes with us, by nature. In the retailing of words, the best becomes overlooked and forgotten.
360

To experiment is a part of nature—genius—it is a proper faculty for encountering the sense of nature—and for dealing with its spirit. The genuine observer is the artist—he discerns the meaning and knows from it the past movement of composition, of manifestations: the consequence of experiencing it from within.
361

How few people have the genius to experiment! The true experimenter must have a profound consciousness of nature itself—the more perfect his talents, the more steadily he conducts his process, the greater the accuracy with which he finds and defines the hidden, crucial phenomena. Nature inspires him as though she were his lover, and reveals herself in order to be consummated through him—the more harmonized his constitution is with her. The true lover of nature delineates himself precisely through his skills and his completeness; through the experiments he seeks to reproduce and to simplify, to combine and to analyze, to romanticize and to polarize, and through his inventive spirit seeks new experiments; he seeks through naturally refining or extending his natural senses themselves to select and arrange experiments, through acuteness and clarity of observation as well as through artistic condensation of experiments and observations to completely describe.

The experimenter is only genius.
363

A good physical experiment can be useful for modelling an inner experiment, and is itself a good inner subjective experiment.
363

Descriptions and narratives of physics: when one begins to think about flames, how does one then proceed? Analysis: fiery fumes, fiery vapors—fiery atmosphere, fiery aether, fiery solid, fiery liquid.
364

Not only man speaks—even the universe speaks—everything speaks—infinite languages.
365

Nature is eternal—not the opposite—and nature preserves herself. Whatever is once manifested, that she manifests ever after according to her slow laws. One should seek the past's origin in the spirit.
366

Even fluid is inspired—certainly more so than the solids. It is perhaps with soul as with heat. Gas corresponds with the soul-medium—the ethereal nerves. Intense stimulation—(mechanical or fire-stimulation) produces vapor or liquification. Genesis of the soul-medium—likewise generation of the soul itself.

By this generation, the soul employs the body and perhaps vice versa—mysticism of this operation.
367

All power works in infinity. Where it is not, where there is resistance, it has found an object.
368

Chemical astronomy will become ere long the most remarkable science.
> 369

Singular harmony of chance in atomic systems.
> 370

Those I most trust and understand, I most love meeting.
> 371

Could response to galvanization be any different than one's response to the inner light? Traces, remainders of sensing in the inorganic kingdom.
Stone and matter are the highest: man is really chaos.
> 372

Cloud-production-apparatus *en masse*, in order to bring water to dry regions.
> 373

Enquiry into the question: has nature itself not altered essentially with the increase in human culture?
> 374

Geognosy. The median mountains are the richest area for manifold fossils. The new, peaceful time is less fruitful for the wonderful production and formation of these—therefore in the newer strata of earth fewer minerals are found. Basalt is the chief element.
The first revolutions were simple, but violent—the ground-revolutions. What followed was already formed, manifold. Thereby their products were yielded by stimulation of the multiplicity of forms, masses and colors. The newest revolutions were more revolutions of the surface—they were partial, local; their products were monotonous and were merely subtle variations upon the ancient product. The features of granite are, as it were, diversely organized upon the earth's equator—the

land flattened against itself. They have uniform weather there. In the median mountains the weather is variable—in the flatlands it is more regular again. They have the most sun. The flatlands have, as do the poles, at times more sun than the mountainous lands—but on an average, less. So the surface of the earth forms itself in analogous designs globally—it resembles the cubic globe. As the most steep faces of one mountain and of another are in suitable parallel alignment with their axis, the plains sloping away, so the plains slope away from the steep mountains of all the earth, and away from the South and North poles. These appearances depend upon residual astronomic, geognostic and geogenic relationships.
375

The alignment of the mountain according to the moon's orbit.
Great depths of the deposited lands.
376

III. *Medicine, Psychology*

Poetic physiology. Our lips have many resemblances to both will o' the wisps in [Goethe's] *Märchen* (fairy-tales). The eyes are the higher twin sisters of the lips—the close and open upon a more healing grotto than the mouth. The ears are a serpent, one which eagerly swallows what the will o' the wisps let fall. Mouth and eye have a similar form.[49] The eyelids are lips, the apple is the tongue and the palate, and the star is the throat. The nose is the brow of the mouth, and the brow of the nose is the eyes. Each eye has its chin and cheekbone.
377

Man is of the same substance as that of which the whole of nature is blended—that is, polarized. The world, the human world, is just as manifold as man is. The world of the animals is already much poorer, and so forth, downwards...
378

As the body stands in conjunction with the world, so stands the soul in conjunction with the spirit. Both paths course out from humanity and end in God. Both circumnavigations are required in corresponding points of their path. Both must think of the means—despite the distance—to remain together and to make both journeys commonplace.
379

Sleep is an intermingled condition of the body and the soul. In sleep the body and the soul are chemically bonded. In sleep the soul is proportionately dispersed through the body—man is neutralized. Waking is a more divided, polarized state. In waking the soul is punctuated, localized.

Sleep is the soul's digestion; the body digests the soul. (Withdrawal of the soul's impulse.) Waking is the interwoven condition of the soul's impulses—the body enjoys the soul. In sleep the systems' bonds are loosed—in waking they are attracted.
380

Could every embrace at the same time be the embrace of the whole Pair—just as nature embraces art (a spirit), the child being the combined product of the double embrace?

Could plants, perchance, be the product of a feminine nature and a masculine spirit—and animals be the product of the masculine nature and a feminine spirit? Are plants perhaps the girls of nature, and animals the boys?

Or are embryos the product of root-generation—plants of the generation to the second power—animals of the generation to the third power-and humanity of the generation to the nth power, or to infinity?
381

Shouldn't a marriage truly be a long, continuous embracing Generation—true nutrition—forming an harmonious mutual essence?
382

The essence of sickness is as obscure as the essence of life.
383

One could call every illness an illness of the soul.
384

Each illness is a musical problem—the healing a musical solution. The shorter and more complete the solution—the greater the musical talent of the physician.
Sickness demands manifold solutions. The selection of the most appropriate solution determines the talent of the physician.
385

Medicine must become something wholly different. The teaching of the art of living and of the nature of life.
If life is really of the highest importance—only then one can hope for an explanation of the complete functioning of all individual physical members. The completed physics will be the universal teaching of the art of living.
Apportioning of life's problems—successive solutions.
386

Abundant agitation of the soul—exercises and practice augment the coherence of body and soul, and make both reciprocally sensitive.
387

The physician's art is indeed the art of slaying.
388

How many kinds of slaying are there? The kinds of slaying, as well as the various means of making ill, shed great light on the modes of reviving, of living, and of healing.
389

Death is nothing but the cessation of the alternation between inner and outer attractions—between soul and world. The intermediate member—the product as it were, of both these infinite oscillating vastnesses is the body, the sensitive—or better, the medium of sensation. The body is the product of and also the modification of sensation—a function of world and soul. This function has a maximum and a minimum, and if these are attained, the change stops. Death is naturally twofold. The relation between x and y is fluctuation back and forth. The function, in full, is but fluctuation. The substance of the constitution is capable of dilation and contraction. Death extends, therefore, into unknown remoteness. Ordering one's life is in the strictest sense the true art of forming the constitution and of improving it; the genuine healing art discloses the prescription for preservation and restoration of the special relationship between and alternation of the impulses or factors.

The artist of immortality pursues the higher medicine—the infinitesimal medicine. He practices the medicine as a higher art—as a synthetic art. He observes the value of both factors at once, and seeks to harmonize them—to unite them in one aim. (Could a king, who is at the same time a moral genius, not himself be immortal?) The outer impulse is already as if it were in its boundlessness there, and for the most part is in the dominion of the artists. But how humble is the inner impulse in comparison to the outer! A gradual propagation of the inner impulses is thus the chief concern of the artists of immortality. With what right can one not say here that which the poet has truly said with singular wisdom—that the muses alone give immortality? Now even the learned class appears in a new light. My magical idealism.

The general medicine is handwork, by calling or guild.[50] Its only usefulness is in this sense. Every sickness, every wound should be employed toward, should be a means toward knowing an ulterior, higher aim.

390

Man must not become accustomed to a more vigorous impulse alone, but must rather progress to even faster oscillations. Both of these viewpoints are part of the artist's teaching of immortality.

391

The soul is by all poisons most strongly affected. The soul's is the most forceful, the most diffused impulse— All soul-workings are therefore gravely damaged by localized evils and inflamed illnesses.

392

A new view of physiognomy—as a prosody of the Inner, and of its relations.

393

Whoever sees everything as spacious, figured and plastic, his soul is musical. —Forms appear through unknown oscillations. —Whoever sees tones and movements in forms, his soul is plastic—because the diversity of tones and movements arise only through figuration.

394

All passions end themselves in tragedy. All that is partial ends in death—so it is with the philosophy of perception—the philosophy of imagination—the philosophy of thought. All that lives ends in age and death. All poetry has a tragic face, a tragic tension. (True jesting is at heart earnest. Tragic working of farces, of the marionette plays—the colorful life—the common and trivial.)

395

The temper of a word points to musical proportions in the soul. The acoustics of the soul are still dark and obscure, but perhaps of a very momentous scope. Harmonic and disharmonic oscillations.[51]

396

When one is truly hungry, one can help oneself through diversion to other attractions. Thus express your need or illness often—your attraction—in a wholly foreign way, through another organ, through another need or inclination. Man is bound to life with many cords or attractions, the lower nature through fewer.

The more induced life is, the higher it is.[52]

397

Anger is a vehement unwillingness. Enthusiasm is a forceful willingness. (Sorrow is perhaps an intense counter-impetus—delight an intense impetus.) All apathy stems from deficiency—(Deficiency of will; deficiency of accomplishment.) In every true illness is a deficiency—and therein originates the aversion toward every illness.

Therefore one asks: How do you feel?

398

Pain and anxiety signify the soul's dreaming aspect. Bodily pleasure and aversion are dream-products. The soul is only partly awake. Where it dreams—as, for example, in the involuntary organism—to which classification in reflective hindsight the whole body belongs[53]—there one perceives pleasure and aversion. Pain and desire are sensations of the bound soul.

399

Sorrow is the symptom—the humor of secretion—the delightful symptom of partaking—the nutrition.

400

Shouldn't more of our feelings—be sympathetic with the pains and affects of particular limbs?

401

On the musical nature of all association and fellowship—Could musical relationships be the source of all delight and aversion?

402

Ecstasy—the inner light phenomenon proportionate to intellectual understanding.
403

The dream teaches us a remarkable way of intruding the faculty of our soul into each object—each in itself instantly transformed.
404

The dream is of the highest significance for the psychologist—even for the historian of humanity. The dream has contributed much to the culture and the formation of humanity—Therefore the ancient great authority of the dream exists with good reason.
405

Patience is twofold: peacefully bearing deficiencies, and peacefully bearing excesses. True patience creates a greater elasticity.
406

To dance—to eat—to speak—to collectively perceive and to work—to be together—to hear, see and feel—all are conditions and inducements and themselves functions—the effect of the higher—the wholly human—the Genius.

Theory of ecstasy.[54] Love is that which draws us together. In all the diverse functions of life is ecstatic desiring (sympathy) for the Ground.[55] The truly delightful function (sympathy) is the most mystic—all but absolute—in other words, the chemicals induce the Totality (mingling) of Union.
407

It is peculiar that the association of ecstasy (*Wollust*), religion, and the ferocity of the people has not long since been made, considering their inner kinship and the familiarity of the tendencies.[56]
408

On carnal lust—the yearning after the touch of flesh—the pleasure of the nude human body. Could it be a hidden appetite for human flesh?
409

The heartfelt contentment which the Waters give—the ecstasy of mingling Waters.
410

On the mystic limbs of man—only to contemplate them—only to move them silently—is already Bliss (*Wollust*).[57]
411

What for the soul is Allure, for the spirit is Beauty.[58]
412

In the same way that we manipulate our brain, our thinking organ, into whatever movement we like—its movements modified at will—doing that and observing the product—and creating meaningful expression—in the same way that we bring the brain's motion to language—as we utter it through conduct—in action expressed, as we voluntarily stop and move ourselves—our movements united and separate—in just the same way must we move the inner organs of our body, to restrain, to learn to unite and to separate.[59] Our whole body is by all means capable of being ruled by the mind. The working of the emotions—the fears, pain, anger, envy, shame, joy, fantasy and so forth—is indication enough. But moreover, one has the plentiful examples of those masters over the individual involuntary parts of their bodies, those who have revived the shunned parts of their bodies. When each will become his own physician—he will be able to acquire complete, certain, and sufficient consciousness of his own body. Not until then will man become truly independent of nature, perhaps even capable of restoring lost limbs; he shall learn how, through will, to slay himself, and thereby to attain the true illumination of the body—soul—world—life—death and the spiritual world. It may be that only he has the

ability to impart life to matter. He shall compel his sense to produce the Form he demands—and he shall live, in a real sense, in his world. Then he becomes capable of separating himself from his body, when he finds it for the best—he becomes able to see, to hear, and to perceive—what and how and in whichever connection he will.
413

IV. *Philology and Art*

The common language is natural—the written language is artistic.
414

Everywhere lies a grammatical mysticism, at the root of which appears to me—could very easily lie the primal astonishment over speech and writing. (The wild folk still prohibit modern writing, deeming it witchcraft.) A disposition toward wonder and mystery is nothing but striving after the supersensual—spiritual attraction. Arcane mysteries are nourishment—of incipient power or potencies. Solutions are elucidated secrets.
415

The letter is what a temple or a monument is: apart from meaning it is certainly dead. —(On the metaphorphosis of the spirit in letters.) There is a spiritual historian of letters—an antiquary philologist. (The antiquary is in truth a restorer of letters—one who restores them from the dead. Use of letters.)
416

All that we experience is a message. So the world in act is a message—revelation of the spirit. Time is no more, where the spirit of God is comprehensible. This sense of the world has been lost; we are subsisting upon letters. We have lost the presence beyond appearance. The Form of Reality.
417

Is language indispensable for thinking?
418

Language is Delphi.
419

Doesn't language also have its treble, bass and tenor tones? Nor also its measure, nor its keynote—nor meaningful stops and tempo? Are not the diverse genre diverse Instruments?
420

Our soul must be airy, for it knows music, and takes pleasure in it.
421

The musical proportions seem to me particularly correct natural proportions.
422

Shouldn't all plastic formation, from the crystalline to the human, be acoustic—be explained by congealed motion? Chemical acoustic.
423

The Arabesque, the Ornate, the Ornamental are uniquely visible music.
424

Music and rhythm. Periodic hexameter—in the grand style. Grand rhythms. Those in whose mind this grand rhythm, this inner poetic mechanism has become indigenous, write involuntarily, enchantingly beautifully, and it appears simply, the highest thoughts associated and drawn together in rich and meaningful order by these singular oscillations, the profound sense of which is just like that of the ancient Orphic sage, whose inspiration came from the wondrous music which is the mysterious pattern, the shaper and soother of the world. We gain here a profound, enlightening insight into the acoustic nature of the soul, and find a new resemblance between light and thought—for both are intermingled oscillations.

425

One can note regarding style, whether and how much the subject of an author attracts or not—and one can make inferences regarding the author's constitution, by way of his chosen voice and so forth.

Full style—meagre style. Bland style—colorful style. Meaningful—monotonous style. Sick, healthy—weak and energetic style.

Healing methods—educational methods of styles.

426

Thus sculpture is nothing more than musical figuristics.

427

Poetry is prose in the hands of an artist. Words are acoustic configurations of thought.

428

All method is rhythmic. If one has the world's rhythm down, then one has the world down. Each individual has a particular rhythm. The rhythmic sense is genius.

Fichte has simply disclosed philosophy's rhythm, and expressed verbal-acoustics.

The true rhythmic nature is sensitive. The individual relationship between sensitivity and the stimulus is the rhythm of individual health. Inasmuch as these proportions are incorrect, so the inadequate rhythms produced will be noxious, unhealthy figurations and concatenations.

429

One must be inspired through unceasing free reflection. In one who has devoted no time to reflection, to free meditation, to tranquil contemplation, and to observation in different voices or

humors, in him the fruitful imagination sleeps, and the meaningful inner realm is suspended. For the poet nothing is more useful than a contemplative perspective of most everyone's worldly concerns, and their characteristics, as well as of the diverse sciences.
 430

 What's more, one can treat business poetically. But to accomplish this transmutation, one needs a profound poetic understanding. The ancients understood this wonderfully well—for how poetically did they describe vegetables, machines, houses, tools and so forth.
 A certain archaism of style, a correct placement and ordering of the whole, a delicate implication through allegory, a certain strangeness, reminiscence, metamorphosis, all glimmer through a given style of writing—these are the unique essential consequences of this art, which I have noted for my bourgeois novel.
 431

 Letters should be restorative, and I should also work with them in this way. Evening's letters—easy, free, romantic, meaningful—preparation for the novel.
 432

 Books are a modern kind of historical reality—but a highly meaningful one. They are perhaps taking the place of tradition.
 433

 Poets are both insular, and lead poetic streams.
 434

 It is highly understandable why, in the end, all becomes poetry. Doesn't the world, in the end, prove to be heart-felt spirit?[60]
 435

 One seeks, with poetry—as if it were only a mechanical

instrument to that end—to bring forth the inner Voice and Vision, and perchance even the spiritual Dance as well.

Poetry is like an art of the emotions.
436

The poet understands nature better than a scientific mind.
437

Clear understanding conjoined with warm imagination is the true, health-bringing precious food of the soul.
438

Poetry must never be substantive, but rather always only wonderful.
439

One should describe nothing which one hasn't fully surveyed, clearly examined, and of which one isn't wholly master—for example, description of the spiritual.
440

Epic, lyric and dramatic are the only three elements of any poem—a work is only chiefly epic when epic emerges as the superior element, and so forth.
441

One must write as if composing.
442

All pure comedic characters must be, as in the delightful ancient plays, coarse and harshly drawn—the fine nuances are prosaic. In the sphere of poetry all is defined—each function is highly alive—and springs colorfully to life before one's eyes.
443

Shakespeare is more obscure to me than the Greeks. The

merriment of Aristophanes I understand, but that of Shakespeare has been a mystery to me for a long time.
444

Earnestness must glimmer cheerfully; jokes must glower soberly.
445

The art of estranging in a given way, making a subject strange and yet familiar and alluring, that is romantic poetics.
446

There is a special sense for poetry—a poetic tuning in us. Poetry is a personal vista, and therefore inexpressible and indefinable. Whoever doesn't immediately know and feel what poetry is—he has no conception of producing it. Poetry is poetry. It is as different from rhetoric as day is from night.
447

Nature has an artistic instinct—when one distinguishes between art and nature, therein lies babbling.
448

Elements of Romanticism. The object must be there—like the tone of the Aeolian harp of old, all at once, without apparent cause—manifested without the instrument.
449

Higher mysticism of art. —As the arrangement of destiny, as natural phenomena.
450

The truly simple, human and romantic is spoken only of God.
451

In fairy-tales is my heartfelt spiritual vision best expressed.
452

A fairy-tale is truly like a dream-image—apart from its conclusion. An ensemble of wonderful things and occurrences—a musical fantasy—the harmonious effect of an Aeolian harp—nature itself.
453

Poetics of evil.
In general, doesn't the best begin in sickness?
Half sickness is evil—whole sickness is delight—and doubtless higher.
Beyond the alluring sickness of evil.
Or does one gather the evil in the world to oneself to annihilate it, like the wicked?[61] Should something in poetry annihilate aversion, as the moral annihilate the wicked?
Do those of good heart pass over to Purity—don't the wicked go there? —No, save through Philosophy.
There are none who are absolutely wicked, and there is no absolute evil.
—It is possible that man himself gradually creates absolute wickedness—and so gradually creates absolute evil—but both are artificial products—which man's moral and poetic laws should utterly annihilate—one shouldn't believe evil—one shouldn't accept it.
Only through opinion (which, when derived from faith, is creative knowledge) does evil arise and endure.
The subject and the object should be (but are not) one—and are bound to become united—as the visibly, objectively base will become subjectively evil, and the visible, subjective evil will become objectively wicked, until they become united and therefore, *ipso facto*, the pure poet abolishes both, because the one annihilates the other itself.
Already from a stable level of consciousness no evil now

exists—and this level of consciousness should become permanent.

Thus even from the philosophical standpoint of the ordinary consciousness, all untruth, as the ground of evil, should certainly be annihilated—which annihilation takes place precisely because the philosopher seeks to master that higher standpoint, and to make it finally stand alone.

Through the annihilation of evil, the good will be realized, introduced, dispersed.

All evil and baseness is isolating (it is the principle of separation) and through union the separation will be annulled and not annulled—but the base and evil as visible separation and union shall in Act, through true separation and union, through these only be overcome and transcended.

I annihilate baseness and evil through philosophizing—exalting—turning baseness and evil back upon itself with goodness and delight, which is exactly reversing the Fall of man.
454

The fairy-tale is, as it were, the canon of poetry—everything poetic must be fairy-like. The poet prays to chance.
455

The genuine fairy-tale must be prophetic description—idealistic description—absolutely essential description. The true fairy-tale poet is a seer into the hereafter.

(With time history must become fairy-tale—it will be again as it began.)
456

Nothing is more opposed to the spirit of fairy-tales than a moralistic fate—a fixed conclusion. In fairy-tales there is a natural anarchy. The abstract world—the dream-world—following from the abstraction of the condition after death.
457

Poetry is the youth below those who know. As a child inclined to descend passes an angel under the Madonna, whose warning finger is pressed to her mouth, so the wise are not comfortable with the poet's thoughtlessness.
458

At the heart of all ideals lies a variation from the usual rule, or a higher, circuitous rule.
459

V. *States and Human Patterns*

History. The Bible begins magnificently with Paradise, the symbol of youth, and closes with the eternal Kingdom—the holy State. Even its two main components are genuinely great history. (In each great history must lie, as it were, the same great story symbolically rejuvenated.) The beginning of the New Testament is the second, higher Fall of Man—and the beginning of the new period. Each human history should be a Bible—should become a Bible. Christ is the new Adam. Idea of rejuvenation, of rebirth. A Bible is the highest order of writing.
460

We are all bound to be transmuted into a You—into a second I—only thus can we elevate ourselves into a greater I—the One and the All are conjunct.
461

The complete citizen lives wholly in the state—he has no possessions outside the state.
462

That is the single attraction of the republic: that everyone in it is outwardly very free. Virtue and vice, courtesy and crudeness, spirit and ignorance, talent and incompetence therefore manifest more strongly, and so a republic resembles a tropical climate, only not in the uniformity of its weather.

463

Man has a state in order to allow him to search for a cushion—and thus the state should be the direct opposite. —It should be an impetus toward complete activity. Its aim should be that its people be made mighty, not utterly weak—not to support them, but rather to make them heroically real.

The state does not excuse man from labor, but rather increases his labors almost infinitely—not freely—that is, without increasing his power to infinity. The way to peace goes only through the temple of all-embracing action.

464

If permanent bonding had introduced for all Cantons the same compositional form, they would have been long since destroyed , and all the faster, the more exactly uniform—the more artificially organized they would have been. The rule of nature is an infinite meaningfulness in forms—unity in principle, which encompasses everything. Müller's history of Switzerland.

465

A man urgently needs a state. In order to become human and to remain human, one has need of a state. The state naturally has rights and obligations, like the individual man. A man without a state is a barbarian. All culture arises from the relationships between the man and the state. The more educated, the more a member of a cultured state. There are wild states—there are well-bred states—moral and immoral—cultured and Philistine states. Acculturation and education of the states. States engender themselves, or are born from other states.

466

Absolute equality is the highest feat—the ideal feat—but isn't natural. By nature men are relatively similar—which is the ancient dissimilarity—the stronger have an even stronger right.

Hence humanity is not freed by nature, but is rather more or less bound by it.

Few humans are human—therefore the rights of man appear outwardly unbecoming, as they really become existent and established.

Be human, that you are able to receive human rights yourself.

467

One must treat the whole earth as ONE estate, and learn from its economy. Nations must finally, truly realize that the attainment of all their aims is possible only through complete, collective principles.

Alliance systems. The approximation of a universal monarchy.

468

Through the individual the estate is ennobled—just as through marriage corporeal delight is ennobled.

469

What is really cosmopolitan, and cosmopolitan interest?

470

The direct consequence of simplicity in one's statutes is the difficulty of the morality in *praxis*.

471

Value of the trifling in morality (macrological and micrological morality).

472

The opposite of love and spirit is one of the strangest and most dangerous—great historical role of this opposition.

473

The more spiritual and cultured a man is, the more personal

are his limbs—for instance, his hands, his eyes, his fingers, and so forth. The application of antiquity, of physiognomy, of the singular realization: that each member must give its specific contribution to the propogation of a man.
474

There are people with headstrong and eccentric tendencies who are not made for marriage. Married people must have a way of mixing independence and non-independence. They must have firm character as the main thing, in order to be able to hold firm—and yet be flexible, elastic, and throughout certain, without being obstinate and anxious.
475

Human patterns. A child is a visible, grown love.
We ourselves are a visible, grown seed of the love between nature and spirit, or art.
476

VI. *Cosmology and Religion*

The brains—the thinking organs—are the world-producers—nature's genitals.
477

Sensitivity and sensibility stand in analogous relation to the body and the soul—or the world and the spirit, or man. The world is the macroanthropos. There is a world-spirit, as there is a world-soul. The soul should become spirit, the body become world. The world is still not ready, so slight is the world-spirit. From a God should come an All-God. From a world should come an All-world. Common physics, higher physics. Man is common prose—he is bound to become higher prose—all-encompassing prose. Formation of the spirit is at the center of formation of the world-spirit—and also at the center of religion. The spirit becomes formed through the soul—and so the soul is nothing other than bound, enclosed, contracted spirit... Formation of the soul is also at the center of formation of the world-soul—and thus indirectly is a religious obligation.

478

Wonderful powers of the bodily appearance—the beautiful lineaments—the form—the voice—the complexion—the musculature and elasticity—the eyes, the sense of touch, of feeling—the outer nature—the angles—the closed-off spaces—the darkness—the veil. Through the selection of clothing the body becomes yet more mystical.

479

In praise of the mysterious state. The unknown is that which attracts one toward knowing. The known attracts no more. The absolutely unknown is equivalent to absolute attraction. Practically I. The possibility of knowledge is itself the highest attraction—the absolute unknown. The unknown Beyond in the sciences. Mystification.

480

On the lovemaking of the soul with the body—
481

The communal madness ceases to be madness, becoming magic, madness according to rules and with full consciousness.
(Poets, madmen, holy ones, prophets)
The possibility, the capability of bringing forth willed sensation. (Faith is the intention of bringing forth such sensation.) (Bound with the knowledge of the absolute reality of the sensations.) If we were blind, deaf, and senseless, our soul, on the contrary, would be completely open, our spirit beyond the now outer world, then would the inner world come to exist with us in proportion as we are now in the outer world, and who knows whether we could truly differentiate?—if we could compare both conditions. We would thus come to feel so very much, by virtue of the absence of light, sound, and so forth. We

would be able to bring forth only variations—the thoughts would be similar, and we would feel a striving to overcome each sense, which we now name outer senses. Who knows whether directly afterward, through manifold striving, our eyes, ears and so forth, could be brought forth?—because as our body thus would stand in our power—it would be made a part of our inner world, as now our soul is. Our body is not permitted to be absolutely senseless—as little as our soul is now. Who knows to what extent the body only appears senseless?— because it makes up only a part of ourselves. And the inner self-division, whereby the body would first see, hear, and feel—without affecting the continuation and the manifestation of the world remaining without—that operation through which we perceive ourselves in a manifold way—-would be very arduous. Here would also arise an absolute, practical and empirical 'I.'

This perspective can widen yet further. We would already appear senseless in that condition, because the soul of the transcending one, of all watchfulness in excitability, would be nurturing potency—just as we now often don't see, hear and feel if our soul is enlivened, our watchfulness alone draws us, and so vice versa.[62]

Free will and chance are elements of harmony. Voluntary and accidental world. In both conditions, the corresponding proportion.

Wonder world and natural world.

Spiritual realm and actual world.

Freer exchange between these two conditions. Free will and chance are one. Wonder and lawful, regular workings. Nature and spirit equal God.

482

The world has a primordial, spontaneous capacity to be enlivened through me—it is, on the whole, *a priori* enlivened by me—one with me. I have a primordial, spontaneous tendency and capacity to animate the world. —I can now live in relation to nothing—which isn't directed by my intention, or isn't in accord with it. Consequently, the world itself must have the primordial capacity to direct itself according to me—and to be in accord with my will.

483

Art of becoming all-powerful. Art of realizing our intentions totally. We must receive the body as the soul in our dominion. The body is the instrument for the formation and modification of our world. We must therefore seek to form our body as a wholly capable organ. Modification of our instrument is modification of the world.

484

In I—at the point of freedom, in the act, we are all indeed fully identical—from there on each individual separates himself. I is the absolute complete space—the central point.

485

With the correct formation of our will the formation of our capacity and knowledge manifests as well. In the instant in which we are completely moral, we become able to perform wonders; it is where we would do no wonders that is morally highest. (Vide Christus.)[63] The highest wonder is pure act—an act of free determination.

486

And a wonder has the world begun.

487

Magical knowledge arises, according to Hemsterhuis, through the application of the moral sense to the remaining senses—i.e.—through the moralization of the world, and of the remaining sciences.[64]

488

Everything in the outer world alludes to mysticism. If all humanity were a pair of lovers, then the distinction between

mysticism and non-mysticism would fall away.
489

Beauty and morality are very much like light and warmth in the spiritual world. One comes to know them through exact information, through relationships to them, through analogies of them, as through scientific information about the stars one is able to position oneself and to describe them, so likewise through information about the spiritual realm one positions oneself and describes it.
490

The philosopher is to the intellect, that is, in the strictest sense, what the poet is to faith.
491

Magic is like art—to willfully use the sensual realm.
492

Theory of persons. A true, synthetic person is many people together—is a genius. Each person is a seed of an infinite Genius. Each is capable of dividing into many people; nonetheless, each is one. The true analysis of a person as such brings out more people—for the persona can be isolated into many individuals, divide itself, and disintegrate. A person is a harmony—not an alloy, and not a movement—without substance, just as soul, spirit and person are one. Each personal expression belongs to a certain person. But all personal expressions are part of the undivided universal personality, and belong to one or more individual personalities together.
493

On nature as a closed body—as a tree—whereon we are the bleeding buds.
494

What is nature? An encyclopedic, systematic index or Plan of our spirit. Why should we, with only this disclosed index, be satisfied with our wealth? It is left to us to examine—and to cultivate and use in manifold ways.

Fate, which oppresses us, is the sustenance of our spirit. Through the expansion and formation of our activity we ourselves become, in fate, transmuted.

Everything appears to flow toward us here, because we don't flow from here outward. We are negative, becuse we will—the more positive we become, the more negative the world becomes to us here—until in the end there will be no more negation, but rather we will be all in everything.

God wants Gods.

495

Our body is none other than a general, central focus for our senses—we have mastery over the senses—we are capable of transmuting by way of activity—to center the commonplace, so all depends upon us alone—a body given to us to do what we will.

Yes, just as our senses are nothing other than modifications of the mind, the thinking organ—the absolute element—so we, through mastery of these elements, become able to modify and to conduct our senses as we please.

496

If thoughts can't be made perceptible (and voluntary) to you, then do the reverse, making external things intentionally perceivable. —which is tantamount to this: if ideas of external things aren't possible, make external things thoughts. If you can't make a thought independent from you, detached—and strange to you—in other words, making the soul externally manifested—then proceed to attempt the opposite with external things—and exchange these mentally.

Both operations are idealistic. Whoever has both completely

in his grasp is a magical idealist. Shouldn't the completion of both operations be dependent upon one another?
497

Magic of the star-like power.[65] Through it man becomes as powerful as the stars; he is, above all, related to the stars.
498

The physical magus knows how to enliven nature and how to deal with it as with his own body—voluntarily.
499

Man should be a complete and total instrument of the Self.
500

Teachings of the spirit. The spirit world is already disclosed to us in effect—it is always manifest. We may suddenly become, however, elastic as necessary to see into the midst of it...
501

Cosmology. It is immaterial whether I place the cosmos in me, or myself in the cosmos. Spinoza placed all outside; Fichte placed all inside. So it is with freedom. Freedom is in the whole as freedom is in me. I term freedom necessity, and necessity is in the whole as it is in me, and *vice versa*. Very many questions of this kind are due, no doubt, to misconceptions of philosophy in general. First I must come to know what an object truly is, so I can subsequently be usefully served by it.
502

The inner world is almost more mine than the outer. It is so heartfelt, so private—man is given fullness in that life—it is so native. A pity that it is so dreamlike, so precarious. Must straightness then be best, when the real is such fiction, and fiction seems so genuine and Real?
503

We are at once in and out of nature.
504

Teaching of the future. Nature will come to be moral if she, from the truer love of art, to art surrenders—and does what art will—and likewise, when from a truer love of nature, art lives for nature, and works according to nature. Both must will together from themselves—and by a stranger choice, from the other. Each must encounter itself in the other, and the other in itself.

If our intelligence and our world harmonize—then we are like God.
505

As for the infinite Greatness, it must give unending Wisdom, unending Humanity, unending Morality, unending Gods. Heterogeneous things can only approximate one another.
506

Prosaic nature of the present heaven and the present earth. World-period of the useful. World-judgement—beginning of the new, refined, poetic period.
507

Axiom: we can of ourselves know nothing. All true wisdom is given us.
508

Whoever has no sense for religion, must nevertheless have something in its place, which is for him what religion is for another—and therein originates much contention. Because both subjects and senses must have many similarities, each employs the same words for its side; yet both are wholly different—so that much confusion must arise.
509

Still there is no religion. —One must first found an associa-

tion (*Bildungsloge*) for a more genuine religion. Believe—in order that religion give. Religion must be created and manifested through the union of ever more people.
510

Spinoza is a man drunken in God.
Spinozism is a supersaturation in the Godhead. Unbelief is a deficiency of the divine organ and of the Godhead.
511

Among the ancients, religion was surely that which among us it must become—practical poetry.
512

Everything which will emanate from God comprises the teachings of the human future. Each machine that now operates in perpetual motion, is bound to be perpetual motion. —Each man who now lives in and through God is bound to become God himself.
513

They are fortunate people who can perceive God everywhere—find God everywhere—these people are uniquely religious. Religion is morality in highest dignity, as Schleiermacher has so excellently put it.
514

Theodicy.
If Good and Evil had their individual merits, so would their conjoining be very much desired.
515

No case in the history of religion is stranger than the new idea in nascent Christendom: one humanity, and one general religion—therein originated proselytizing.
516

Ordinarily, I must have superstition in Jesus. (Superstition is in general essential to religion—as one commonly believes, that is.)

517

The Christian religion is notably strange, in that it accepts the simple good intentions in humanity—our inherent nature—placing value upon our nature for what it is, without special training. In this it stands in opposition to science and art and individual delight.[66]

It proceeds from the common man.

It inspires the great majority of the dull, the narrow-minded, upon earth.

It is the light which begins to gleam in the darkness.

It is the seed of all Democracy, the highest aspect of popularity.

Its unpoetic exterior, its resemblance to a modern domestic painting, appears to be only borrowed.

It is tragic and none the less infinitely mild—a true drama—a combination of comedy and tragedy.

The Greek mythology appeared to be for the educated classes—and so appears to be the absolute opposite of Christianity.

Pantheism is a third end.

518

Our whole life is a divine service.

519

There is no religion that couldn't have been Christian.

520

On the concept of prayer. Prayer is in religion what thinking is in philosophy. To pray is to create religion. —Sermons should truly be prayed. The religious sense prays—like the mind thinks.

Religion comes out of religion—it has a characteristic religious world, a characteristic religious element.
521

Why can no virtuosity occur in religion? Because it rests on love. Schleiermacher has proclaimed a kind of love as religion—an artistic religion—a religion nearly like that of the artists, who revere beauty and the Ideal. Love is free—it most happily chooses the poorest and most helpless.

God himself named the poor and sinful as his most beloved. There are loveless natures, as there are irreligious ones.

Religious duty: to have compassion along with the Godhead.[67]

Infinite sadness of religion. As we are bound to love God, so he must require our help. To what extent is this duty lost to Christianity?

Love of the loveless object. Incarnation of humanity. Inclination of Christ toward the Moral.
522

Through religion humanity first becomes truly one.
523

We are bound nearer to the unseen than to the visible.
524

God is love. Love is the highest reality—the ur-ground.
525

II. Selected Poetry

The Stranger

January 22, 1798
Dedicated to Frau Bergrätin von Charpentier

You're weary and cold, Stranger, you appear not
Accustomed to these heavens—warmer breezes blow
   In your homeland, and freer;
      Your young breast longs for former times.

Doesn't eternal spring spread there, in still fields
Colored life all around? Doesn't tranquility stretch there
   Strongly woven, floating? And blooms
      There not eternally, what once grew in abundance?

O! You seek in vain—lost, perished is
That former heavenly land—no mortals
   Know the path on which always lies
      Veiled, the inaccessible ocean.

Few are your kindred folk,
Yet saved from the Flood—here and there are
   Those who are sown and await
      Better times, reunions.

Follow after me willingly—truly a good fate
Has guided you here—familiar companions are
   Here, on the plain, in silence
      Today, to celebrate the homeward festival.

Unmistakable appears there the intimate
Heartfulness—it radiates innocence and love
   Clearly, in all its aspects
      As once it was in your native land.

THE STRANGER

More luminous arises your gaze—truly, the evening's become
Like a friendlier dream, which soon passes you by
   Since in sweet speech
      Your heart dissolves in goodness.

See—the Stranger is here—who from that other land
Feels banned, like you; the hour of lamentation
   Is his; the day of joy
      Wanes early for him.

Yet still he gladly lingers, and where he touches his companions,
Lively, he celebrates the Festival with homeward delight.
   He enchants the spring,
      Which blooms so freshly round the Parents.

O, that the daily Festival oft returns
Ere the weeping ones reluctantly abduct the mother
   And on nightly paths
      Follow the Ruler into the native land.

O, that the enchantment not weaken, that the bond blesses
Your ties—and that the most distanced
   Supports you, and wanders
      A more joyous way with you—

This you wish of the guest—but the poet says
You are for him; then he is gladly silent, for he is joyful
   And he yearns so, even now,
      For his distant lovers.

Stay this gracious stranger—meagre joys are
His, reckoned on earth—still, with such friendly
   People he keeps watch, forbearing
      Until the greater day of birth, beyond.

Fragment

I feel it within me, struggling
A genius, feathers smouldering;
As my sense and heart rise toward the Aether
The body barely fetters me down.

Quo me Bacchus . . .

Fragment of an Horacian Paraphrase

Where do you draw me,
Abundance of my heart,
God of the ecstatic?
What forests, what chasms
I roam over, strangely courageous.
What caverns
Listen
To Caesar's eternal luster
Weaving me into the wreath of stars
And conjoining us to the Gods?
Unheard, immense
No mortal lips let slip
The things I wish to say.
How the glowing, ardent Night-wanderers,
The Bacchae, astonished
Upon the banks of the Hebrus[1]
And in Thracian snow
And in Rhodes, in the wild lands,
Seem so singular, so strange—
Flowing waters,
Lonesome wood.

The Boat Journey

Young man, rowing quickly, hold your rapid strokes;
One each island there, spring dwells
  As Graces dance
    Near Apollo's pleasant play.

See the Sun—it sinks beneath the beeches
Always gently downward in the distant breeze.
  Redness gleams over the knoll,
    Which the evening's blush greets.

Chalice of joy in the kisses of a host of rosy maidens
I look forward to mine in that very place; see, they beckon
already.
  Hesperus should light us
    Until the envious morning star.

Cythere

The best Muse is Cythere;
My incense arises for you no more,
Erato, no longer to you
Is the honor and praise of the poet due.

Since she sent me Luisa, my rhyme
Slips away so sweet and light
As from the rose that I plucked
A butterfly takes flight.

I murmur only rhymes along the stream
As she teaches me of love and nature,
And under myrtle[2] when I dream
Then I dream only songs.

The Dying Genius

Welcome, loved one, now and not again my voice
Calls you; near is my departure.
   I have found that which I sought
     And the bonds of enchantment melt.

The lovely Being—you see the Queen—
Lifts the ban, the spell. How long in vain I hovered
   About the Throne, until at last
     Through her beckoned my ancient home.

Already that secret ember glows, intense
My old Essence—deep in the earthly
   Creation: you should be sacrificer
     And sing the song of the return.

Take the branches, cover me with them,
Toward the East, then, sing the exalted song
   Until the Sun ignites, rising,
     And opens the gates of the primal world for me.

The fragrance of the veil which once encircled me,
Sinks then, golden, across the plain—
   And whoever breathes its scent vows inspired
     Eternal love to the beautiful princess.

Almighty Spirit, Source of All Being

Almighty Spirit, Source of All Being,
Zeus, Ahura Mazda, Brahma, Jehova
Before the First Aeon you already were,
As after the last Aeon you still are there.
Out of desolate darkness you call brilliant Light,
As out of the wildest Chaos, an Elysium, bright.
You gesture, and look! A Temple turns to Hell
As a Sun is enveloped, all around, by Night.

From your mouth flows life and vitality
Into Sirius; into this tree.
And nourishment you emanate
To myriad tiers, joyous delights.
A child calls to his father to dine
Even if he'd been a thousand days sated
On a stream of food and wine
His father'd bestowed unbidden and unabated.

Why should I, your child, never voice a plea
For the nourishment already given me—and
For the shimmer of higher reality
With which soul and body come alive,
With which don't you the sacred, hornèd man revive?
Give me, Spirit, Creator, the higher silence of the soul,
Vanquish abysmal pain; delight and fortune impart.
Give me the wisdom to always choose true gold,
And fill to abundance this feeling of the heart.

Know Yourself

There is only one, which people of all times have sought in vain,
  Everywhere—now in the heights, now in the very depths of
    the world—
But under diverse names, it concealed itself
        always;
  Always one sensed it further—never quite able to grasp it.
Long ago lived a man who revealed to children in
        familiar myths,
  Way and Key to the hidden Palace.
Though few discerned that simple cryptic watchword,
  Those who did became the Masters of the Way.
Ages passed—the error sharpened our sense—
  Till the myth no longer obscured
        Reality.
Fortunate is the one who becomes wise, who no more
  upon the world
        broods.
  Who longs for the Stone of Eternal Knowledge within.
Only the discerning one is the true adept—he
        changes
  All into Life and Gold—needing Elixirs no more.
In him arises the vapor of the holy Alembic—
    the King is in him—
      Delphi too, and he finally grasps this: Know your
        Self.

                            Freiberg, May 11, 1798

Hymns to the Night

What living being,
Sense-endowed,
Loves not above all
The wondrous appearance
Of the diffused spaces about him,
The delightful Light—
With its colors,
Its gentle utter presence
In the Day?
As life's innermost soul
It breathes the restless
Vast and starry world
Which flows dancing in its blue flood.
It breathes the glittering stone
The tranquil, suckling plants
And the animals,
Manifold,
Ever-active power—
It breathes the many-colored
Clouds and breezes
And above all
The majestic Stranger
With the portentous eyes
The floating movements
And the resounding mouth.
As King
Of the earthly nature
It summons every power
To uncounted transformations
And its presence alone
Reveals the wondrous mastery
Of the kingdoms of the earth.

Downward I turn,

Toward the holy, unspeakable
Mysterious Night—
The world lies distant
As if sunken in a deep vault.
How desolate and lonely
Is her place!
Profound sadness,
In the depths of my heart, I ache.
Distant memories,
Wishes of youths
Childhood dreams
Brief joys
And fruitless hoping
Come in grey clothing
As evening mist arises
After the Sun sets.
Distant lies the world
And its bright satisfactions.
In other spaces
The delightful canopy
Of Light is disclosed.
Shouldn't it come anew
To its true Children,
To its gardens,
To its majestic house?

But what arises
So cool and invigorating
So full of portent
Beneath our heart
And absorbs
The sadness' gentle breath?
Have you taken
A human heart,
Dark Power?
What do you hold
Under your cloak

That slips, unseen and powerful
Into my soul?
You only appear frightening—
Precious balm
Falls from your hand
From the poppies you hold.
In sweet drunkenness
The great wings of the spirit lift you aloft
And fill us with joy
Dark and unspeakable,
Secret, as you yourself are,
Joy that foreshadows
A heaven to us.
How poor and childish
The light seems to me
With its colorful things,
How delightful and blessed
The day's departure.
Because the Night
Estranges you from your servants
You sow
Luminous spheres
In vast spaces
To make your omnipotence known
Your turning anew
In the times of your withdrawal.
Heavenly as flashing stars
In each vastness
Appear the infinite eyes
Which the Night opens in us.
They see further
Than the most distant glow
Of that uncountable multitude
Needing no light
They see through the depths
Of a loving mind, a heart
Which fills the highest spaces

With unutterable Ecstasy.
Praise the Queen of the World
The highest messenger
Of the holy world,
The one who nurtures
Holy love.
You come, Beloved—
The Night is here—
My soul is enchanted—
The earthly day is past
And you are mine again.
I gaze into your deep dark eyes
And see nothing but love and ecstasy.
We sink upon the altar of Night
Upon the soft bed—
The veil drops
And kindled by your heated touch
The flame of the sweet offering
Glows.

II.

Must morning always come anew?
Does earthly power never end?
Must wretched activity consume
The heavenly approach of Night?
Will the hidden offering of love
Never burn eternally?
To light was appointed
Its time
And its watching—
But timeless is the majesty of Night
The duration of sleep is eternity.
Holy Sleep!
Don't bless too seldom
Night's consecrated ones—

Only the foolish mistake you
And know of no sleep
But those shadows
Which you compassionately cast over us
As that twilight
Image of the real Night.
They don't feel you
In the golden fluid of the grape
In the almond tree's
Wondrous oil
And in the poppy's brown juice.
They don't know
That it is you
Who hovers over
The delicate girl's breast
And makes a heaven of her womb—
They do not suspect
That from the ancient tales
You appear, to reveal heaven
And you carry the key
To the dwellings of the blessed,
Infinite secrets
Of the silent messenger.

III.

Once, lost, I shed bitter tears—
    There my hope was dissolved in pain
and I alone stood upon the parched hill which
buried the Form of my life in dark, constricted Space,
Solitary—how I was lonesome—agitated by unspeakable
anxiety, powerless, possessed with only wretched thoughts—
It was as if I could see help nowhere, neither before nor
behind me—and fled, extinguished was life, with the
endless suspense of longing—Then there came from the blue
distances,

From the heights, my ancient ecstasy: a twilit tremor
>> awe—
And the bonds of birth were rent, the
Fetters of Light—Back fled the earthly masters and
my sorrow with them. Sadnesses flowed together into
an unfathomable world—You night raptures,
Heavenly slumber came over me.
The scene itself gently rose higher—my unbound, newborn
Soul soared over the scene. The hill became a dust
>> cloud
and through the cloud I saw the clear features of my Beloved—
In her eyes rested Eternity—I grasped her hands
And the tears became a glittering unbroken bond.
A thousand years passed by in the distance
like cloudbursts—Upon her neck I wept the enchanted,
delighted
tears of that new life. That was the first dream in you.
It lingered long, and its reflection
endured as the eternal, unshakeable Trust
in the heaven of Night and its Sun, the Beloved.

IV.

Now I know when the last morning will dawn—when
the Light will no longer shun the Night and Love—
when all will dawn as eternal slumber and one sole
inexhaustible
>> Dream
Heavenly weariness oppresses me again.
Long and laborious was the way to the holy Grave
and the cross was heavy. But whoever's lips are moistened
by the crystalline wave alone, the hidden imperceptible
thoughts which well forth from the hill's dark womb
to break upon the foot of the earthly flood, whoever has
stood on this sure boundary to the world and
seen beyond, into that new land, into Night's throne,

truly doesn't travel back into the strife of the world,
into that land where light and detestable, ceaseless
unrest rules. Aloft, he builds himself a tranquil shelter,
where he takes refuge, longing and loving, gazing beyond
until that most welcome of hours when he attains
The well of Origins. Everything earthly
floods up and becomes
the Highest, spiraling downward, and what was holy through
Love's touch flows in hidden channels as a fragrant essence
where it mingles like clouds with the sleeping lovers.
Still you awake
Merry light, you awake—
The weary to work—
To infuse me with that joyful life.
But you can't entice me
From the memory
From fading, mossy thoughts.
Gladly I will
Engage my fleet hands
Looking everywhere
For what you might require
And praise your radiance
So brilliant
And seek to reveal
The beautiful symmetry
Of your artful works
Gladly regarding
The pregnant courses
Of your forceful,
Luminous hours,
The ground of your power
The harmony and proportion
The wondrous Play
Of unutterable Space
And its times.
But my secret heart
Remains true to the Night

And her daughter, creative Love.
Can you show me one
Eternally true heart?
Has your Sun
A friendly glance for me?
Can the stars clasp
My extended hand?
Do they return
Its gentle pressure?
Have you adorned them
With colors
And brilliant outlines?
Or was
Your adornment
To give a higher, more esteemed Worth?
    Which delight,
    Which satisfaction,
Offers life
That outweighs Death?
Doesn't everything
Inspire us
To bear the colors of Night?—
She bears *you*—motherly,
And it's her you can thank
For all your mastery.
You would have fled
into yourself
Into endless space
Blown apart—
If she hadn't held you
And bound you
So that you were hot
Blazing
To engender the world.
Truly, I was long before you were
With my kind,
Sent from my Mother

To dwell in your world
And make it holy
with Love.
To give human sense
To your creation
Which still ripens
With the thought of God.
Still the traces
Of our presence
Are few.
One day your hour will approach
The end of time
When you will fulfill
Our one and only longing:
To be extinguished and to die.
I feel in me
The stirring of the end
The heavenly freedom
The blessed calm of home.
In wild sorrow
I know your distance
From our home
Your resistance
Against the ancient mastery
Of heaven.
But your wrath
Your fury's in vain.
Incombustible
Stands the cross
Triumphant sign
Of our kind.
    I journey beneath it
    And each pain,
    Once a thorn,
    Becomes delight.
Still, for a time
I am lost

And rest drunken,
Your love in my heart.
Infinite life
Comes over me.
I see from higher
Down to you.
On every hill
Dawns your glow.
A shadow precedes
The cool circle.
O! Absorb, Beloved,
My power
So I can eternally
Sleep
And love.
I feel Death's
Rejuvenating flood
And impatiently await in the Storm
With faith and courage,
Night-death,
Holy-fire.[3]

V.

The scattered human tribes
Were ruled for ages
By an iron destiny,
Mute force.
A dark and heavy bond
Lay upon
Their timid souls.
Endless was the earth.
The Gods resided
In their home:
A realm of jewels
And majestic wonders.

Since eternity
Its mysterious Form
Stood among the morning's
Blue mountains;
In the ocean's
Holy womb
Dwelt the Sun
The all-pervading
Living Light.

An ancient giant
Bore the blessed world;
Fast beneath the mountains
Lay the primal sons
Of Mother Earth,
Impotent
In their destructive rage
Against the newly
Reigning Gods
And their intimates
Joyous humanity.
The dark ocean's
Blue depths
Were a Goddess' womb.
Heavenly ones
Dwelled in joyous delight
In the crystalline grottos—
Rivers and trees
Flowers and animals
Had human senses.
Sweet was the wine
Which the blossoming young Gods
Gave humanity—
The golden corn's
Full sheaves
Were a gift from the Gods

In love, drunk with joy,
A holy service
Of heavenly beauty.
So life was
An eternal celebration
Of Gods and men.
And childlike,
Every generation
Revered the precious Flame
As the highest in the world.
Only one thought jarred:
The dread of leaving that joyous table
Enveloped the soul in wild terror.
Here even the Gods could give no advice;
For the heart filled with sweet trust
Mysterious was this malevolent path.
This thing that raged beyond supplication, and which no gift stilled—
It was death that cut short
These delightful festivals with anxiety, pain and tears,
And which continually separated everything.
Here the heart was stirred by sweet ecstasy—
There it was severed from the Beloved.
In vain they longed: great misery shook them—
The imminence of their deaths only caused dispirited dreams,
A weak, unconscious struggle against its imposition.
The wave of delight was shattered
Upon the rocks and crags of infinite chagrin.
With daring spirit and the glow of higher senses
Men embellished the inhuman ghoul,
Imagining a pallid youth dousing the light, and stillness—
Gentle is the end, they said—like the tone of a harp—
Memories quietly immersed in the cool flow of phantoms.
The poet sang of sad want,
But still eternal Night remained without remedy
For the somber sign of that distant power.

The ancient world waned
The garden of delight
The young tribes
Withered—
And out
Into the distant spaces
Strove the growing
Unchildlike people.
Vanished were the Gods.
Nature stood
Lonely and lifeless
Bound by harsh numbers
And iron laws.
And in conception
As in dust and breath
The inconceivable blood dissolved
Into the thousandfold lives.
The omnipotent Trust
Took flight
With her all-transmuting
Intimately joining
Heavenly companion:
Fantasy.
A cold North wind
Cruelly blew
Over the barren waste
And the wondrous world
Vanished into the Aether.
And into heaven's
Infinite distance
Filled with the lustrous world
Into its deepest holy places,
Into the heart of the highest spaces,
The soul of the world withdrew
With her powers
To wait for the dawn
Of new days

And the higher destiny of the world.
No more was light
The Gods' abode
And heavenly symbol—
They cloaked themselves
With the veil of Night.
Night was
The manifestation
Of the fruitful womb.
Then, amid a people
Despised by all
Too early ripened
Among whom the blessed innocence of youth
Became strange, defiant,
A new world appeared
With its unseen countenance
In poverty,
In a marvellous shed—
A Son of the First Mother,
Mysterious offspring
Of Infinite fruit.
The Eastern lands'
Prescient, full-blooded
Wisdom
First knew
Of the dawn of the new age.
A star guided the path
Of the Kings
To the humble cradle.
In vast future names
With glitter and fragrance
And the highest wonders of Nature
They honored him.
Alone unfurled
The heavenly heart
Toward the love,
The glowing womb

Of the Father's compassionate countenance—
And rested on the gentle breast
Of the loving Mother.
With godlike ardor
The knowing eye
of the blossoming child
Gazed into future days
After his Beloved,
The offshoots of his divine self,
Unconcerned with the days
of earthly conflict.
Soon he gathered childlike hearts
About him,
Wondrous moved
By his pervading love.
Like flowers there arose
A new, strange life
Around him—
Inexhaustible words
Joyous tidings
Fell like divine sparks
From familiar lips.
From the distant shores of Hellas
Born of serene heavens
Came a singer
To Palestine
And gave his whole heart
To the wondrous Child:
> You are the youth who in ages past
> Stood upon our graves in deepest reflection;
> A consoling symbol in the darkness
> Higher humanity's joyous beginning.
> We were sunken in profound sorrow
> And you drew us up with sweet longing.
> In death eternal life is known—
> You are death, and first to make us well.

The singer went

Full of joy
Toward Hindustan.
His heart was filled
With eternal love
And poured out
Fiery songs
And under each gentle heaven
The intimate
Of the earth inclined
Toward him;
A thousand hearts
Nestled close
And the joyous word
Arose a thousand fold.
Soon after the poet departed
The precious life became
An offering for the human's
Deep disease—
He died young,
Torn
From the beloved world,
From the weeping mother
And from his friends.
The unutterable suffering,
The dark chalice
Emptied by the holy mouth
In bitter anguish.
Near was the hour of birth
Of the new world.
Fiercely he fought with that ancient horror—death;
Heavy lay the grasp of the old world upon him.
Once more he cast a familiar glance at his Mother—
Then came the eternal love
His hand went slack—
And he slept.
For only a few days
A dense mist hung over

The raging ocean;
Over the black and quaking earth
The Beloved wept
Uncountable tears.
Then the mystery was revealed:
The heavenly spirit raises
The primal stone from the dark grave—
Angels watch over the slumbering Form
Lovely dreams
Fragile symbol.
He ascends in new Godhood
And awakens in the highest,
The rejuvenated, newborn world.
He buries with one hand
The ancient dead world
In the desolate abyss
And lays with immense power upon it
The stone which no power can move.
Still the lovers weep
Tears of joy
Tears of tranquility
And of infinite thanks
Upon your grave.
They always see you—
Joyously afraid, they see you
Resurrected.
They see you
Weeping on your Mother's
Blissful breast
And with your friends'
True hearts wander—
Speaking words that fall
Like leaves from the Tree of Life.[4]
You hasten with full longing
Into your Father's arms
Bringing the young
Childlike humanity

And the Golden Age
Of inexhaustible drink.
The Mother soon hastens after
In heavenly triumph—
She was the first
To enter the new realm
With you.
Ages passed
Since then
And always in higher brilliance
You rule the new Creation
And raise thousands
From pain and grief
Full of trust and longing.
All are true to you
And reign with you
And the heavenly virgin
In the realm of Love
And serve in the Temple
Of heavenly Death.

The stone has now been lifted
Humanity has arisen—
With you we now endure
And feel no bonds nor prison.
Our harshest griefs now vanish
Before your golden bowl
For earth and life are touching
In this last evening's meal.

Death calls us to the marriage
The Lamps are burning bright
The virgins are here, joyful
Of oil there is no slight.
The distance resounds, endless
From your features' light

And the stars now call us
With human voices bright.

For you, Maria, burn
A thousand hearts, alive
In this life of shadows
They yearn for you alone.
They hope to live forever, well,
With prescient delight—
Embrace them, holy Being
To your true breast, to your Light.

So many are there, glowing,
In bitter pain consumed
And in escaping this world
They turn toward you, entombed.
Helpless they appear to us
In great want and pain
Down we come there to them
To shine and never wane.

No one wails beside the grave
For pain, whoever's living trusts;
Those who have this living love
Cannot be robbed, nor treasure rust.
In yearning is their solace
Inspired by deep Night—
By true heavenly children
Their hearts are kept in sight.

In trust our lives progress
Toward eternal life, complete;
Strengthened by the inner glow
Our senses are made clear, and so
The realm of stars will vanish
Into golden life and wine

Which we'll drink and savour
And brilliant, like stars shine.

Love is freely given
And separation's gone;
Our life is filled, complete, alive
Like waves in an endless sea, none strive.
One single night of ecstasy—
An eternal poem, soaring, free—
And our Sun, eternal, bright,
Is the Face of God, the living Light.

VI. *Longing For Death*

Down, down into Earth's womb,
Away from Light's reign,
The pain-filled fury and wild impulses
Signal our happy departure.
Swift our narrow bark
Bears us to the heavenly shore.

We praise unending night,
To eternal sleep—a song.
Well has the day warmed us,
Withered us with sorrow long
Delight in the alien leaves us—
We to our Father's house belong.

What should we do in this World
With our Love and Faith?
The old has been put behind,
And what then can we do
With the new?
O lonely stand, so deeply grieved he
Who devoutly clings to rinds of antiquity.[5]

In ancient times when senses were lit
By flames' high burning,
And the Father's hand and face
Were known to the human race,
The higher sense, so simple,
Still many conjoined with the archetypal.[6]

In ancient times so rich with blood
Primeval branches flourished,
And children longed for heavenly realms
Through sufferings and death.
And though life of delight spoke
Many hearts for love, broke.

In ancient times, in youth's glow
God himself to earth did show, did
To an early death for love's care go—
Sacred his sweet life.
He didn't refuse either fear nor pain
That he might only priceless to us remain.

With anxious eyes we see
In darkest Night enveloped,
And this burning thirst unquenched must be
By all that temporality's developed.
And we must now homeward go
That we this holy Time shall see.

What then keeps us from return?
The departed have already long waited.
The Grave closes our life's sojourn;
Henceforth are we pained, and anxious
We have no more to seek here—
The heart is filled, the world, empty.

Infinite and filled with mystery—
Through us sweet visions stream

And to me from distance's depths
An echo resounds—our sorrow—
The departed seek after us also,
Would send us vision's inspiration.

Down, down to that sweet Bride,
To Jesus, to the Beloved,
Take solace—From twilight
The living, the miserable, take fright.
A dream breaks our bonds apart
We sink into the Father's heart.

Notes and Commentary

NOTES TO THE INTRODUCTION

1) Anthropocentric implies here not the modern sense of man as dominator of nature, of man as ego, but rather the traditional view of man as microcosm, as the one being capable of uniting the realms.

2) *Republic* 527e.

3) For the Persian correlates to this realization, see Henry Corbin, *Spiritual Body, Celestial Earth*, (Princeton: Princeton University Press, 1972). The realization of the *daimon* is by no means unique either to Novalis or to Platonism, for one finds equivalents in Taoism, in Buddhism, in Islam, and in Hinduism, to name but a few. This is not, however, to say that these are all identical realizations.

4) This is not to say that these mystics thought identically, only that they belong to a general current of insight peculiar to Germany, to which Novalis was heir. For translations of Franz von Baader's and Louis Claude de St. Martin's works, see *Avaloka: A Journal of Traditional Religion and Culture*, III.1 & 2, Winter-Summer 1989. These are the only translations of von Baader's work available, to our knowledge.

5) René Gérard, *L 'Orient et la Pensée Romantique Allemande*, (Paris: Didier, 1963).

6) This matter of the irreality (we do not say unreality) of the ego-entity is a very difficult and profound one; in Buddhist teaching it is, in the doctrine of the two truths, held that from a limited or provisional perspective there is an ego-entity (just as there are, on the surface of an ocean, waves) but from a deeper perspective there is no such entity (just as there are no waves deep in the ocean).

7) Virtually every edition of Novalis' aphorisms is numbered differently—therefore, since we compiled this collection from several sources, we numbered the fragments ourselves. These numbers are for this translation alone.

8) By physics, however, he meant something rather different from the modern disciplines, more on the lines of Goethe's elective affinities model perhaps.

NOTES TO THE FRAGMENTS AND APHORISMS

1) Or: 'We seek everywhere the Acausal, and find only the Causal.'

2) That is: when the light of spiritual knowledge has begun to annihilate ignorance, there is a more subtle illness, which must also be erased.

3) The imaginal or visionary power, as the Islamic scholar Henry Corbin noted, is not mere imagination, but is the realization of the higher reality

within oneself as Mind. In Persian Sufism the imaginal realm is *hurqulya*; in Buddhism it is *sukhavati*, or the Pure Land. It is related to the realm of the gods or *devas*—angelic beings—the realm 'nearer' Divine Reality. Novalis is here aligned with the traditional Zen Buddhist understanding: that though one can be reborn amongst gods or animals according to the state of one's mind, one can also turn the visionary *speculum* upon oneself. The realm of the gods, as that of the animals, is according to Buddhism subject to causation and hence birth and death, while man is alone capable of conjoining lowest and highest, of wholly realizing the Real. Man, Novalis is affirming, is capable either of ascending and descending the scale of being, or of turning within and realizing that which is beyond ascending and descending.

4) The grandfather of Charles Darwin, Erasmus Darwin (1731-1802), a British physiologist and poet.

5) That is: the universal spirit, or Mind, is one, and recurs in individual existences. As the Islamic *hadith qudsi* has it: "I was a hidden treasure, and I wished to be known, so I created the world." In Buddhism the reflective or illusory nature of existence is termed 'conditioned reality.' Here the 'reflection' is the glimpse of the Origin mediated through the realm of illusion.

6) This is a re-affirmation of the traditional Hermetic idea of man as microcosm in whom all things are reflected. One can either be bound by the causal—past and future—or, through meditative watchfulness, realize one's inherent indivisibility from all things.

7) Presumably Edmund Burke's eloquent condemnation of the French Revolution.

8) The reference here is to the Platonic Forms, which is to say, to the eternal archetypes existing 'intermediately' between the formless Transcendent and the immanent realm reflecting the Forms. Says Frithjof Schuon: "The cosmic, or more particularly the earthly function of beauty is to actualize in the intelligent creature the Platonic recollection of the archetypes, right up to the luminous Night of the Infinite." *The Essential Writings of Frithjof Schuon*, (New York: Amity House, 1986) p. 377.

9) The suggestion here is that all true knowledge is no more than the remembering of that which was lost when the soul, as Plato among many said, fell into the material realm and was blinded by ignorance. In Sufism, the actual practice of remembering the Divine—centered upon the chanting of the Divine Name—is termed *dhikr*, this corresponding to the chanting of the *nembutsu* in Jodo Shinshu or Amida Buddhism. In a traditional culture activity and learning are valued inasmuch as they further the remembrance of the human Divine Origin, so that in a greater sense one's whole life is a kind of invocation or remembrance, this being the essence of the crafts traditions as well.

10) That is: as a symphony is to an individual performer, so the macrocosm is to the microcosm.

11) Like most of the aphorisms, this works upon many levels. For instance,

dragon-flies—*die Libellen*—means spirit-level as well, in German.

12) The implications of this aphorism are complex: it suggests that one must tread upon false gold while searching for the true spiritual gold by remaining indifferent, like the ocean—yet you should tread upon the firm ground, or you will be overwhelmed by Vulcan. There must be a balance between the throne of the mountain (Vulcan) and the indifferent ocean.

13) In other words, the seemingly loyal clouds—the mountains' constant companions below—in reality not only hid from them their higher origin, but wore them away as well.

14) Perhaps one of the best characterizations of the man of the Tao—though Taoism was virtually unknown in Europe at that time—yet written in the Occident. See the works of John Blofeld and Michael Saso for contemporary discussions of Taoism.

15) The implication of the above passage is that, one who wishes to abandon the complexities of the world in favor of the other, higher world is in fact paradoxically—by maintaining the illusion that there are two worlds—confining himself to this one. Duality is the primal illusion; in truth, *nirvana* and *samsara* are one. Divine Reality shines through this very world.

16) An extraordinarily condensed and allusive observation, the implications of which are that, as in Taoist painting, only the barest outlines (as in a vignette) are necessary to grasp the whole, and moreover, that the briefest phrase may have enormous ramifications. For instance, the ashes of the annihilated illusory self are in truth the pollen which fertilizes and enlivens heaven (the calyx).

17) Literally: *siesta* or *sieste*.

18) That is, as in Taoism: the less the artist exists as a being separate from his work, the more perfect the work. See, for instance, Chuang Tsu's tale of the woodcarver, in which the woodcarver simply allows the work to appear in its perfection.

19) Or 'of the elements.' That is, the inner and the outer—the body and the elements—are one. Both, in the traditional Hermetic framework, are subsumed to soul, which is subsumed to spirit, in the eternal triad.

20) *Wollust*

21) The *Shem Hamephorasch* is the most ineffable of the Kabbalistic Divine Names. At one time worn on the breastplate of Jewish warriors, it is never uttered.

22) Literally: 'fingers' *einen Menschenleib*—a human belly or womb.

23) The sense has been translated; literally, the implication is that man 'squares' while woman 'encircles.' One is reminded of the Hermetic aim of squaring the circle—that is, of uniting the poles.

24) Hetaerae were courtesans in ancient Greece, corresponding in many respects to the *Devadasi* of India, whose tradition survived even into our present century.

25) 'Clothing' is a Kabbalistic term referring to one's Divine raiments, seen upon the shedding of the body, of the earthly garments. It appears also in Sufism in the symbolism of the Angelic journey, on which see Henry Corbin, *Avicenna and the Visionary Recital*, (New York: Bollingen, 1960), pp. 35 ff., 292 ff.; on Kabbalism see Gershom Scholem, *Kabbalah*, (Jerusalem: Keter Publishing House,1984) pp. 132, 133, 147.

26) Cf. *Tao Te Ching*: "A great journey begins with a single step." One implication is that the first step must not be a mis-step, else the journey may be thwarted.

27) That is: the genius in paradise is the condition of separation from passional contingencies; self-knowledge is not annihilation, but absolute awareness uncolored by subjectivity.

28) The lower needs in man correspond to the causal, determinative or passional elements in his nature; the contingent must be overcome in order to realize the transcendent.

29) That is: the two realms are not really separate—we merely imagine them so in order to speak of the Absolute in terms of duality, of discursive consciousness.

30) Novalis is here drawing upon Christian Kabbalism, in which the various possibilities outside the terrestrial human condition are recognized, however incompletely. For a schematic of the possible conditions in which beings may exist, see René Guénon, *The Multiple States of the Being*, J. Godwin, trs., (Burdett: Larson, 1984). In Hermeticism it is said that the being may enter an elemental state, from which it may not 'return'—which is to say, the being irrevocably enters into an inferior condition, losing its human centrality. The condition of 'island' probably corresponds to the solipsism of the being in hell.

31) That is to say: although the Platonic theory of Forms is still valid—being universally valid—we no longer understand it.

32) An ancient religion oriented around worship of the sun.

33) In traditional terms, the planets are not only physical bodies, but more importantly, fundamental principles of existence which man must harmonize.

34) That is: all boundaries are ultimately of our own making. The attainment of the Incomparable requires first the faith that it exists, and second the will to attain it.

35) The concept of the *daimon*, central to traditional Hermetic thought from Egypt, through Greece, and into the Renaissance through Agrippa, Ficino and Bruno, is virtually inseparable from Platonic and Neoplatonic thought. See, for instance, Plato's *Timaeus*, in which each soul is assigned a star—the eternal *daimon* of which we are but a reflection. See also Iamblichus, *De Mysteriis*.

36) That is: regardless of the phenomenal realm in which we find ourselves, Mind—the Sun—is the fundamental reality.

37) Novalis refers to the traditional doctrine of correspondences, in which

each stone, each plant and each animal is seen to correspond with other realms according to planetary categorization, the planets being harmonic aspects of the indivisible web of existence. This is the basis of all traditional medicine, be it Taoist, Paracelsian, or Islamic, to name but a few. See Arthur Versluis, *The Philosophy of Magic*, (London: Arkana, 1986) on this topic.

38) Heaven underlies, is all.

39) This is in fact a Tibetan Buddhist teaching—that the human realm is a kind of ossification from a higher and more 'fluid' station of existence, that before 'history' man, freed as yet from the need for food and physical sustenance, lived for a very long time indeed.

40) Or 'Above time, where birds, animals and trees have speech.' In terms of traditional cosmology, the reference is to the second, celestial realm 'above' the limitations of time and space, corresponding to *hurqulya* in Persian Sufism and to *sukhavati*, the Pure Land, in Buddhism.

41) Novalis here alludes to the Osiris-mythos of ancient Egypt, according to which the God's limbs were severed by Typhon and reconstituted by Isis, on which see Arthur Versluis, *The Egyptian Mysteries*, (London: Arkana, 1988), I.V, 'Osiris.'

42) The implication is that wisdom is beyond all definition and categorization, and hence each philosophical system—as such—can only present various aspects of the incomprehensible. No philosophical system can encompass the whole—or be, in other words, consummate. At the heart of each philosophical system lies the essence of the phenomenal world, which is so far beyond definition that each person conceives of it as something else, perceiving only given aspects of it. Wisdom cannot, finally, be defined—hence no philosophical system can be perfect.

43) Kant's term for the irreducible mode of being in each individual.

44) In Platonic terms, the more the soul is trapped in and blinded by time and space, the more it operates under the illusion that it is separate from the world. Faith is the seed of the realization that what is outside is inside. From the illusion that we and the world are separate arise the 'errors of time and space.'

45) As is taught in Vajrayana Buddhism, certain aspects of Reality are through faith visualized as personified forces, aspects which are, as Novalis said, mediate between oneself and the Divine, and therefore are in a sense more Real than phenomenal reality. Faith is not mere blind belief, but rather knowledge of that not yet realized within oneself.

46) In other words, faith is a channel between lower and higher realms.

47) Novalis is here employing the Scholastic distinction between quiddity and accident, between essential and contingent.

48) Or to paraphrase Novalis: 'Out of the perpetual maw of death arises eternal life.'

49) The geometric form of the mouth and eye is that of the *vesica*, a form

extremely important in Pythagorean geometry in that it signifies the interpenetration of the two worlds, represented by two circles overlapping, as David Fideler has pointed out in his forthcoming *The Song of Apollo.* See also John Michell, *The Dimensions of Paradise,* (San Francisco: Harper & Row, 1988).

50) One might note that in the various traditional civilizations—whether it be Islamic, Christian medieval, or Japanese—the spiritual traditions work along the lines of guilds, and this naturally, for a man's calling is the most natural place for his religious nature to begin. See René Guénon, *Initiation and the Crafts,* (Ipswich: Golgonooza Press, 1980).

51) In traditional thought, from the Pythagoreans to Tibetan Buddhism, words have a sacred quality inasmuch as they arise from and awaken through chanting, the primal higher harmonic aspects and nature of existence. The *mantra* is a phrase above either words or music, signifying and awakening that which within each of us is nearer the Divine.

52) In other words, 'the more needs or hungers, the higher the organism.' A man, obviously, has more needs than a plant.

53) The implication is that the dream of existence arises from the soul being bound in an involuntary organism—the body.

54) Or 'Theory of *Wollust.*'

55) The parallels here with the teachings of Jacob Böhme, the mystical shoemaker, are not accidental; Novalis was an avid reader of that inspired author.

56) One implication is that the masses tend to drag down or destroy the ecstatic, creating a martyr, as discussed in the introduction. This is, however, largely a Western tendency. Another implication is of course that the illusory freedom from self generated in the crowd is a kind of ecstasy; but it is of course a perversion of the religious movement toward transcendence.

57) A reference to awakening to one's angelic counterpart or better, origin—in Greek teaching, one's *daimon,* or genius; in Buddhism the 'body of light,' of which one's physical existence is merely a reflection.

58) Novalis here alludes to the Hermetic doctrine of three worlds, according to which soul is the subtle realm of allure and aversion, and spirit is the transcendent realm of contemplation, hence of beauty.

59) That is: it is possible to attain conscious control over the involuntary functions of the body—for instance, over breathing, heartbeat, and other organic functions. This parallels, of course, the similar abilities of yogis, abilities which have been verified numerous times. Metaphysically, this ability signifies the interpenetration of the higher and lower realms, and their union in the microcosmic individual.

60) 'Heart'—*gemüt*—is closely aligned with 'soul,' 'spirit,' and 'feeling,' and is nearly untranslatable.

61) This thought parallels to some extent the bodhisattvic ideal of Mahayana Buddhism, and may well be related to Lurianic Kabbalism, in which the

holy one was held to redeem the world by drawing evil to himself (even by committing apparently evil acts in order to 'raise the fallen sparks' of God, which are scattered throughout the worlds). See Gershom Scholem, *Kabbalah*, (Jerusalem: Keter Publishing House, 1974) pp. 420 ff.

62) This enigmatic account, which refers to the coming into being of the soul both from the other world into this one, and conversely, the remembering of the soul in the other world, is remarkably parallel to the account of the same procedures in the *Dabistan*, a seventeenth century Islamic compendium of religious practices translated by Shea and Troyer (Tudor: 1937). On p. 398 we find: "there is no doubt of our spirit being the phenomenon which manifests itself in the body from mental excitement and exultation; then it may happen that the spirit receives such a force and perfection that its relation to the world of corruption be like our relation to the body, whence its desire may be the mover in this exterior world." European attention was drawn to this Islamic work by Sir William Jones in 1787.

63) Cf. the story of the Zen Buddhist who was challenged to walk upon water by a magus. "Showoff!" said the Buddhist master, who waded across the river. Also: just as Christ refused to save himself from the cross (the material realm), so the *Bodhisattva*, out of infinite compassion, vows not to abandon samsaric existence until all are freed of its bonds.

64) That is: magical knowledge arises first through whatever knowledge of the other world is latent within one; the cultivation of the moral sense brings it to fruition.

65) For more on the Western understanding of the star-daimon, see Marsilio Ficino, *De vita coelesti*, translated by Charles Boer as *The Book of Life* (Dallas: Spring Publications, 1980), and Plato's *Timaeus*, 41.

66) All of these require training in order to attain skill and appreciation; Christianity, unlike other traditions, demands no spiritual training, only belief.

67) This parallels the Mahayana Buddhist bodhisattvic ideal—that out of infinite compassion the *Bodhisattva* refuses to abandon samsaric existence until all beings have been freed from suffering. Indeed, Novalis' thought parallels, often in a striking way, many Buddhist teachings. At least in part, of course, this is due to the universal nature of truth, or *Dharma*. See, for one view of these matters, Lama Govinda, *The Way of the White Clouds*, (London: Hutchinson, 1966) pp. 147-151.

NOTES TO THE POETRY

1) The river in Thrace—now called the Maritsa—into which, according to Greek legend, Orpheus' lyre and decapitated head were thrown. The lyre was said to continue playing, the head to sing softly, sadly as they floated.

2) A bridal wreath.

3) We have here conjoined certain parts of the hand-written manuscript and

the more standard version of the poem.

4) A line from the version printed in the *Atheneum*.

5) This last section, which in many ways is anti-climactic, coming after section five's ecstatic conclusion, 'pivots' between a longing for the golden age of mankind, and an awareness that, for the present humanity, the golden age cannot be.

6) We wish to preserve here the implications of the 'higher sense' as intellect, which perceives reality in its 'onefoldness' in the archetypal unity of the Father's Mind.

Bibliography

Primary Sources

W. Bölsche, ed., *Novalis' Ausgewählte Werke in Drei Bänden*, (Leipzig: Hesse, 1903)

E. Heilborn, ed., *Novalis Schriften*, (Berlin: Reimer, 1901)

Alfred Kelletat, ed., *Werke und Briefe: Novalis*, (Munich: Winkler, 1962)

Paul Kluckhohn and Richard Samuel, eds., *Novalis: Schriften*, (Stuttgart: Kohlhammer, 1960-)

Hans Joachim Mähl and Richard Samuel, eds., *Werke, Tagebücher, und Briefe Friedrich von Hardenbergs*, (Munich: Hanser, 1978-)

Carl Seelig, ed., *Gesammelte werke*, (Herrliberg-Zürich: Bühl Verlag, 1945-1946)

Gerhard Schulz, ed., *Novalis: Werke*, (Munich: Beck, 1969)

Ewald Wasmuth, ed., *Werke, Briefe, Dokumente*, (Heidelberg: Schneider, 1953-)

Secondary Sources

Benz, Ernst, *The Mystical Sources of German Romantic Philosophy*, B. Reynolds and E. Paul, trs., (Allison Park: Pickwick, 1983)

Birven, Henri Clemens, *Novalis, Magus der Romantik*, (Büdingen: Schwab, 1959)

Feilchenfeld, Walter, *Der Einfluss Jacob Böhmes auf Novalis*, (Berlin: Eberia, 1922)

Frierichsmeyer, Sara, *The Androgyne in Early German Romanticism: Friedrich Schlegel, Novalis and the Metaphysics of Love*, (New York: Bern, 1983)

Gérard, René, *L'Orient et la Pensée Romantique Allemande*, (Paris: Didier, 1963)

Gerhard, Wehr, *Novalis: Ein Meister christlicher Einweihung*, (Freiburg: Aurum, 1980)

Haslinger, Josef, *Die Aesthetik des Novalis*, (Königstein: Hain, 1981)

Heibel, Frederick, *Novalis: German Poet, European Thinker, Christian Mystic*, (New York: AMS, 1969)

Kuzniar, Alice, *Delayed Endings: Nonclosure in Novalis and Hölderlin*, (Athens: University of Georgia Press, 1987)

Mähl, Hans Joachim, *Die Idee des Goldenen Zeitalters im Werk des Novalis*, (Heidelberg: Winter, 1965)

von Molnár, Géza, *Romantic Vision, Ethical Context: Novalis and Artistic Autonomy*, (Minneapolis: University of Minnesota Press, 1987)

Müller, Bruno, *Novalis—der dichter als Mittler*, (Bern: Lang, 1984)

Saul, Nicholas, *History and Poetry in Novalis and in the Tradition of the German Enlightenment*, (London: Institute of Germanic Studies, 1984)

Schlumm, Hans, *Blauer Tagtraum, Goldnes Zeitalter bei Novalis*, (Frankfurt: Materialis, 1981)

Senckel, Barbara, *Individualität und Totalität: Aspekts zu einer Anthropologie des Novalis*, (Tübingen: Niemeyer, 1983)

Sohni, Hans, *Die Medizin der Frühromantik*, (Freiburg: Schulz, 1973)

Strack, Friedrich, *Im Schatten der Neugier: christliche Tradition und kritische Philosophie im Werke Friedrichs von Hardenberg*, (Tübingen: Niemeyer, 1982)

PHANES PRESS both publishes and distributes many fine books which relate to the philosophical, religious and spiritual traditions of the Western world. To obtain a copy of our current catalogue, please write:

PHANES PRESS
PO BOX 6114
GRAND RAPIDS, MI 49516
USA